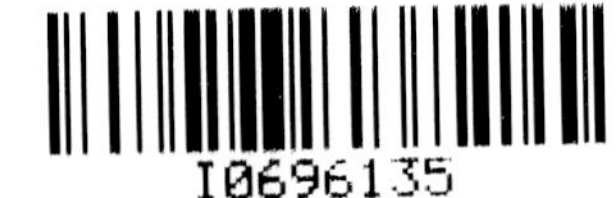

May wisdom guide us to a better world!
God bless you all.

Fabio Silva

2024

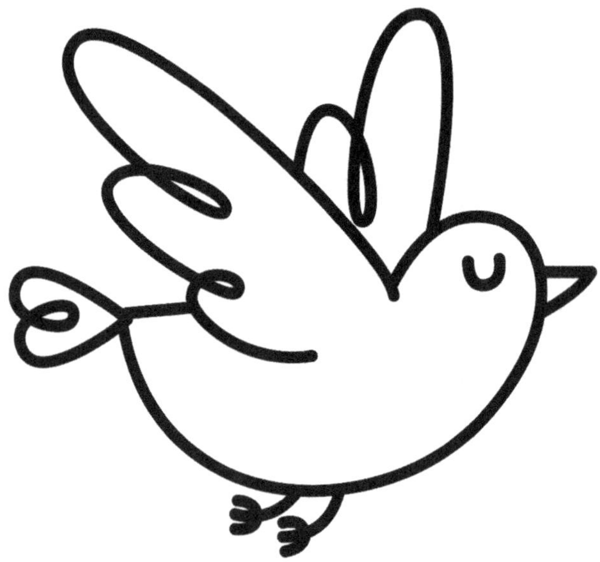

Write your name here

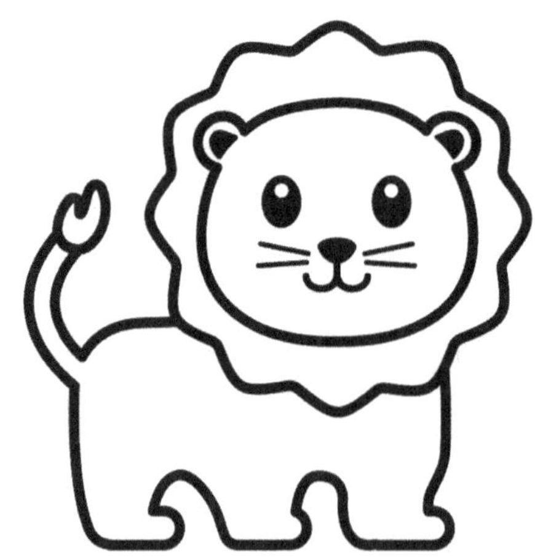

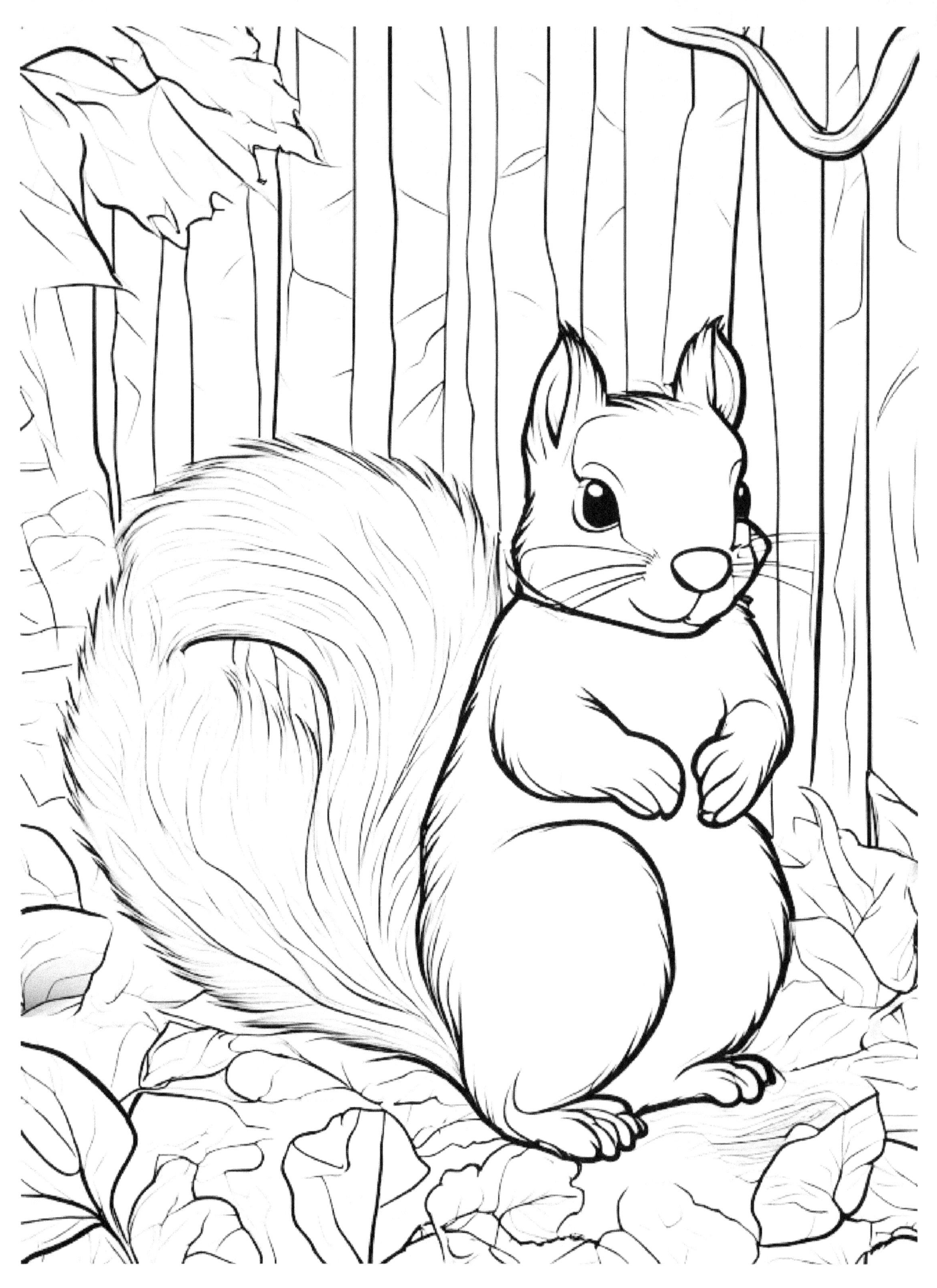

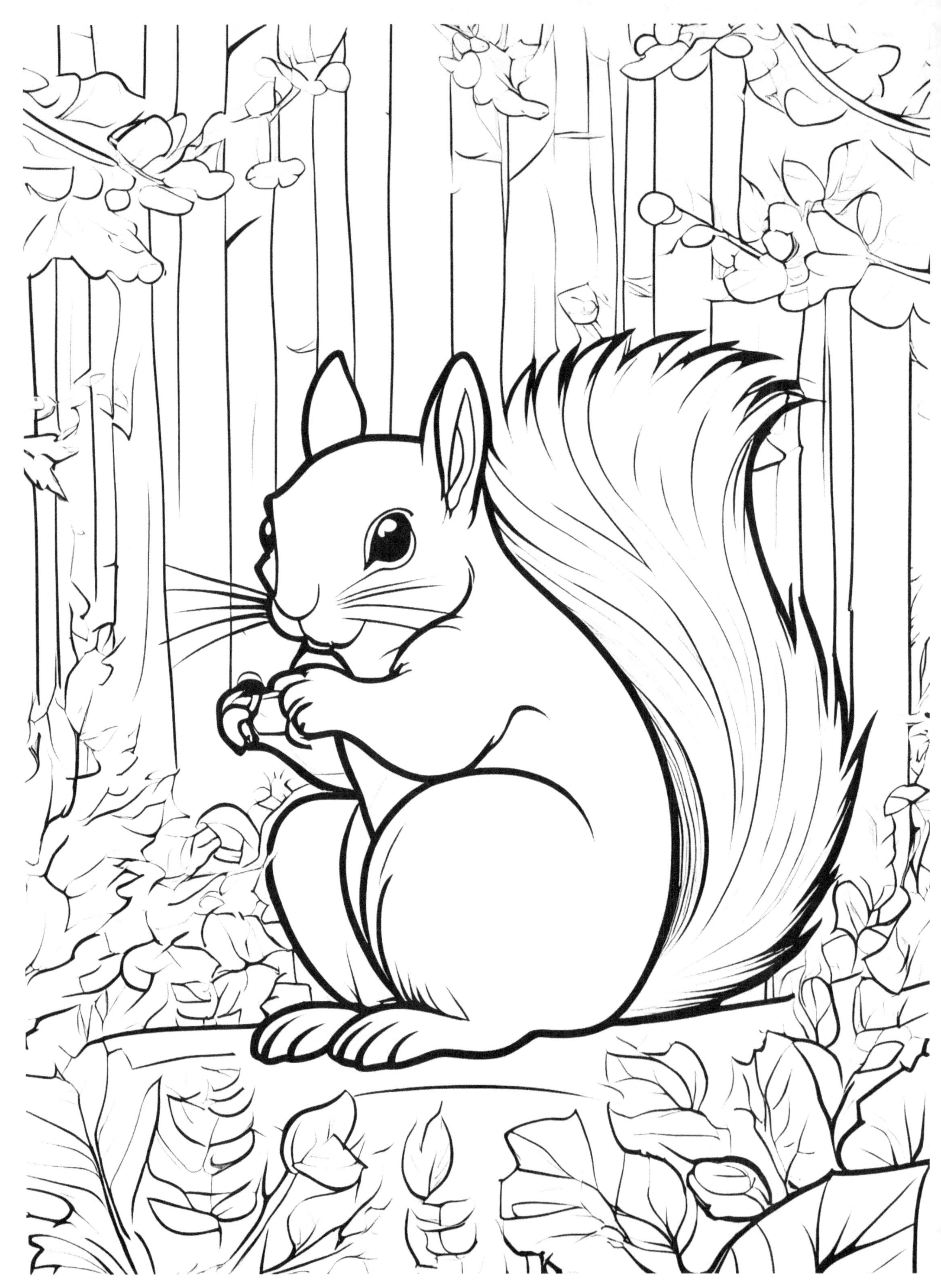

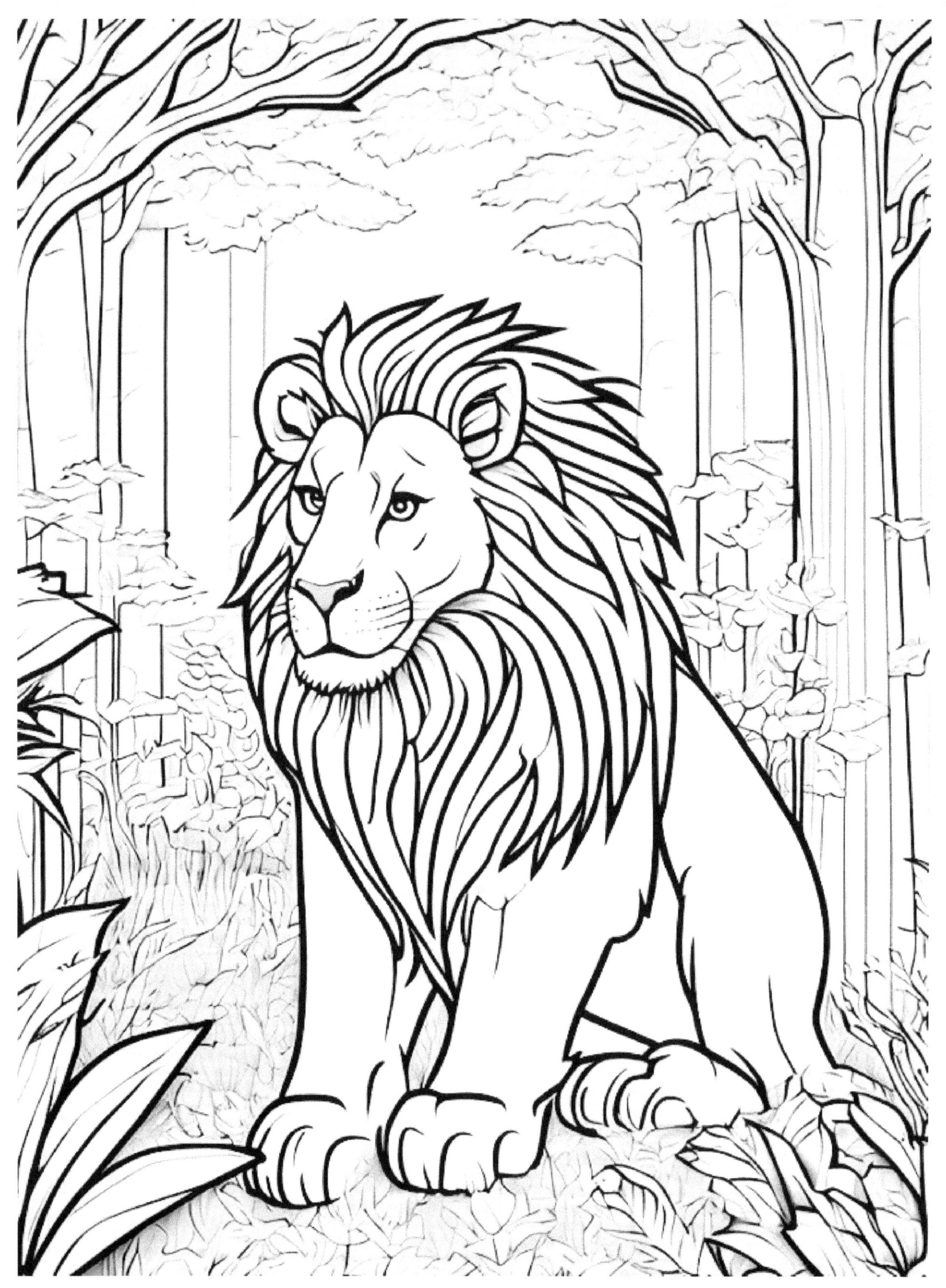

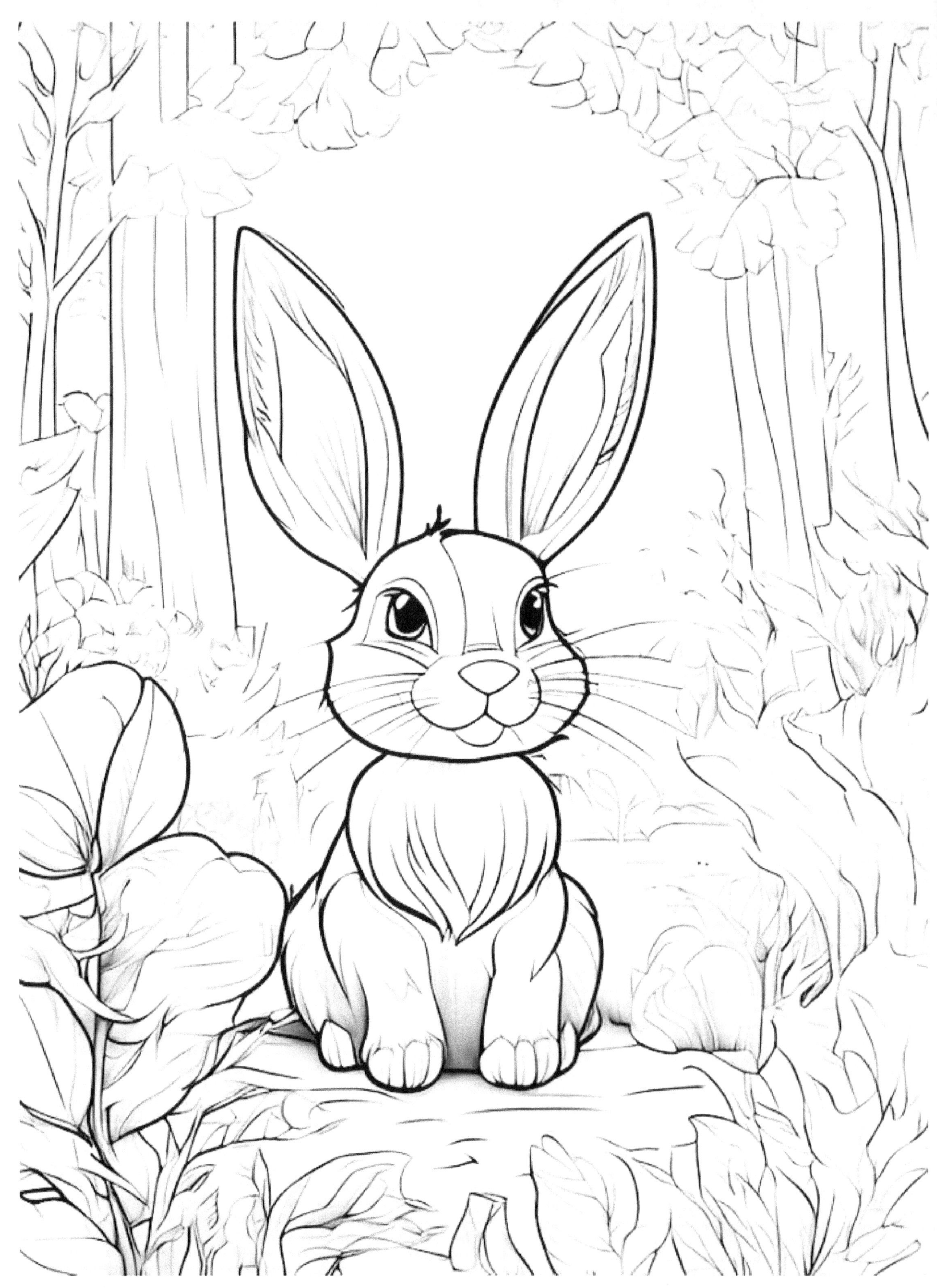

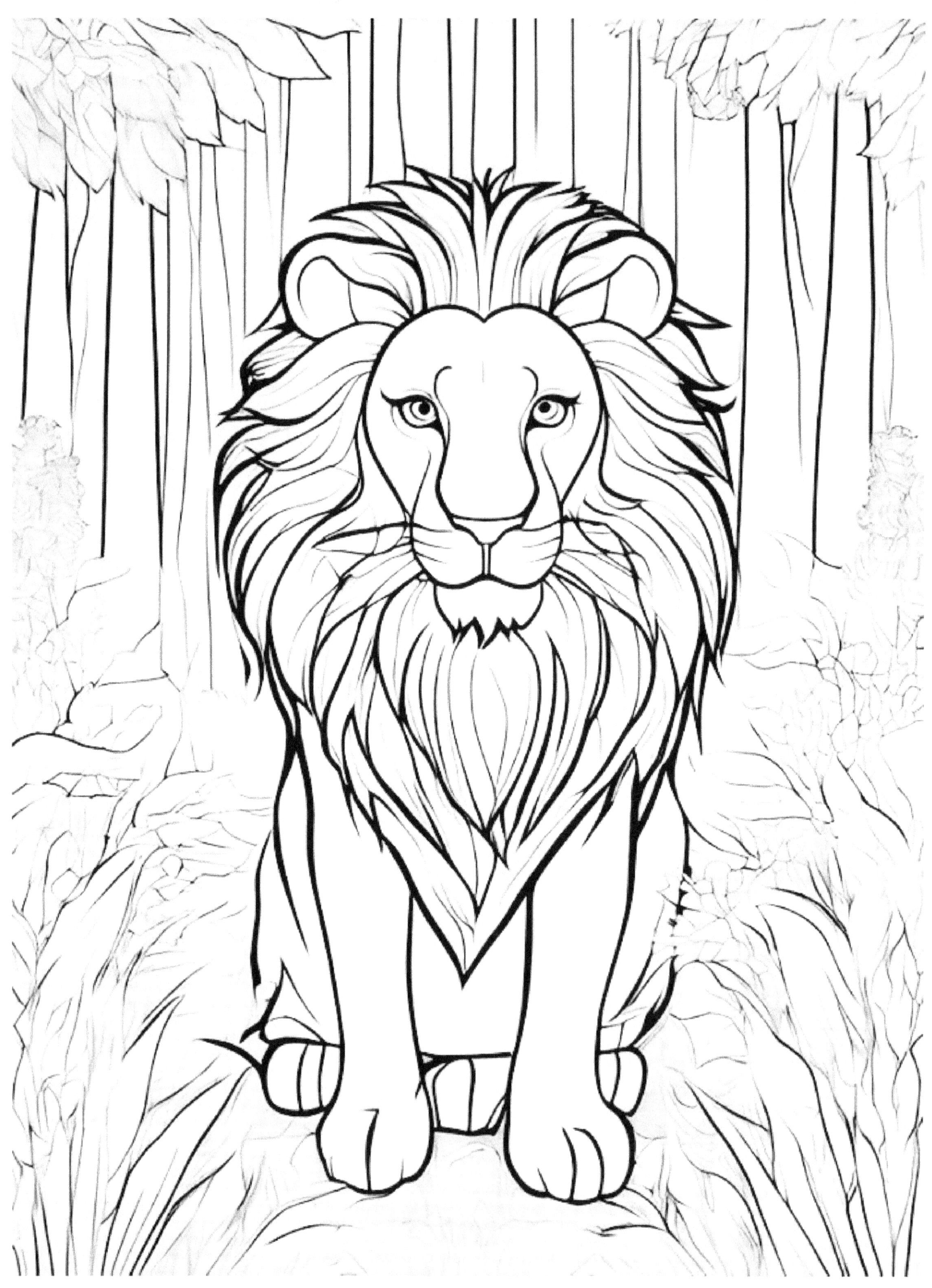

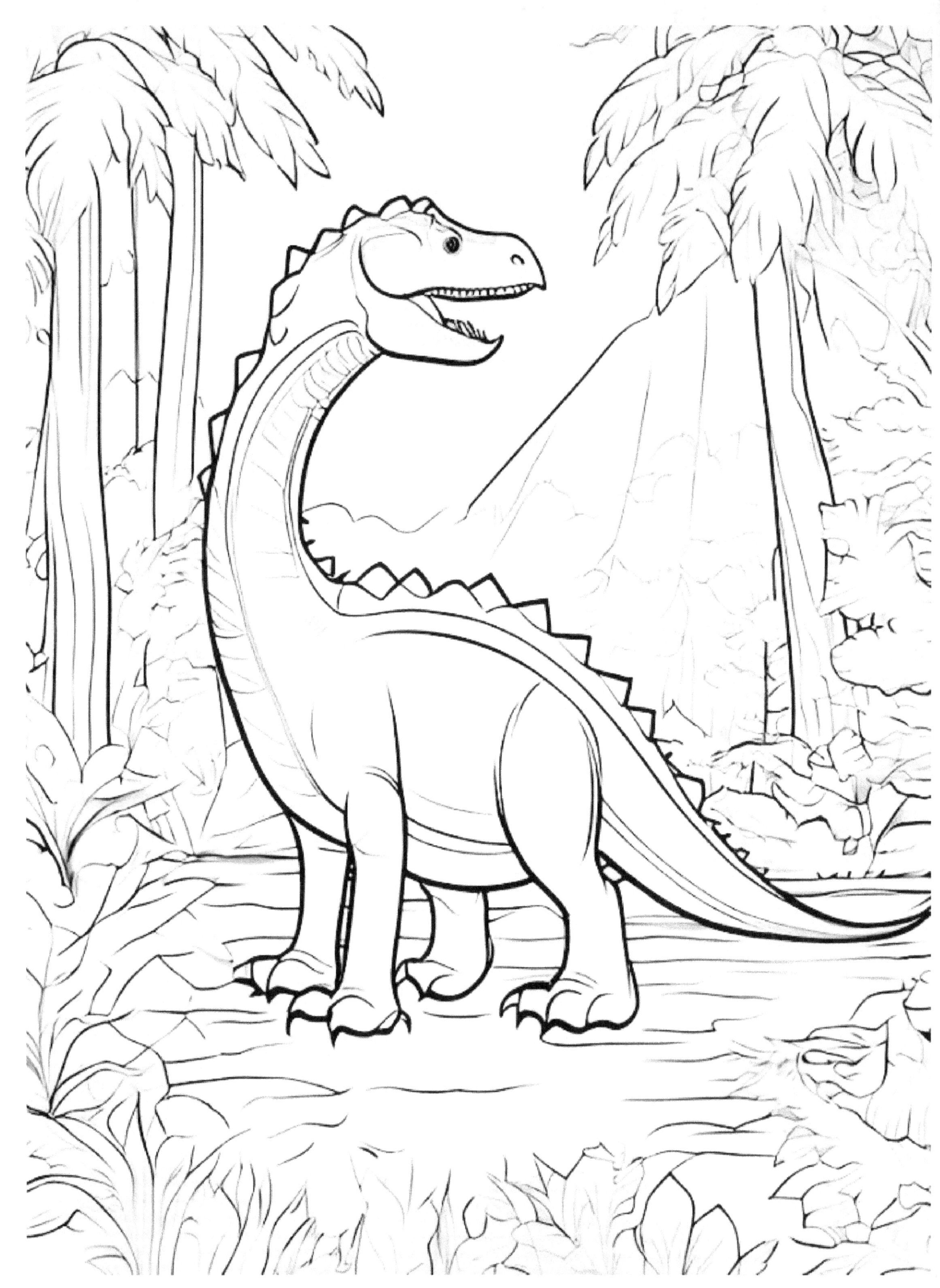

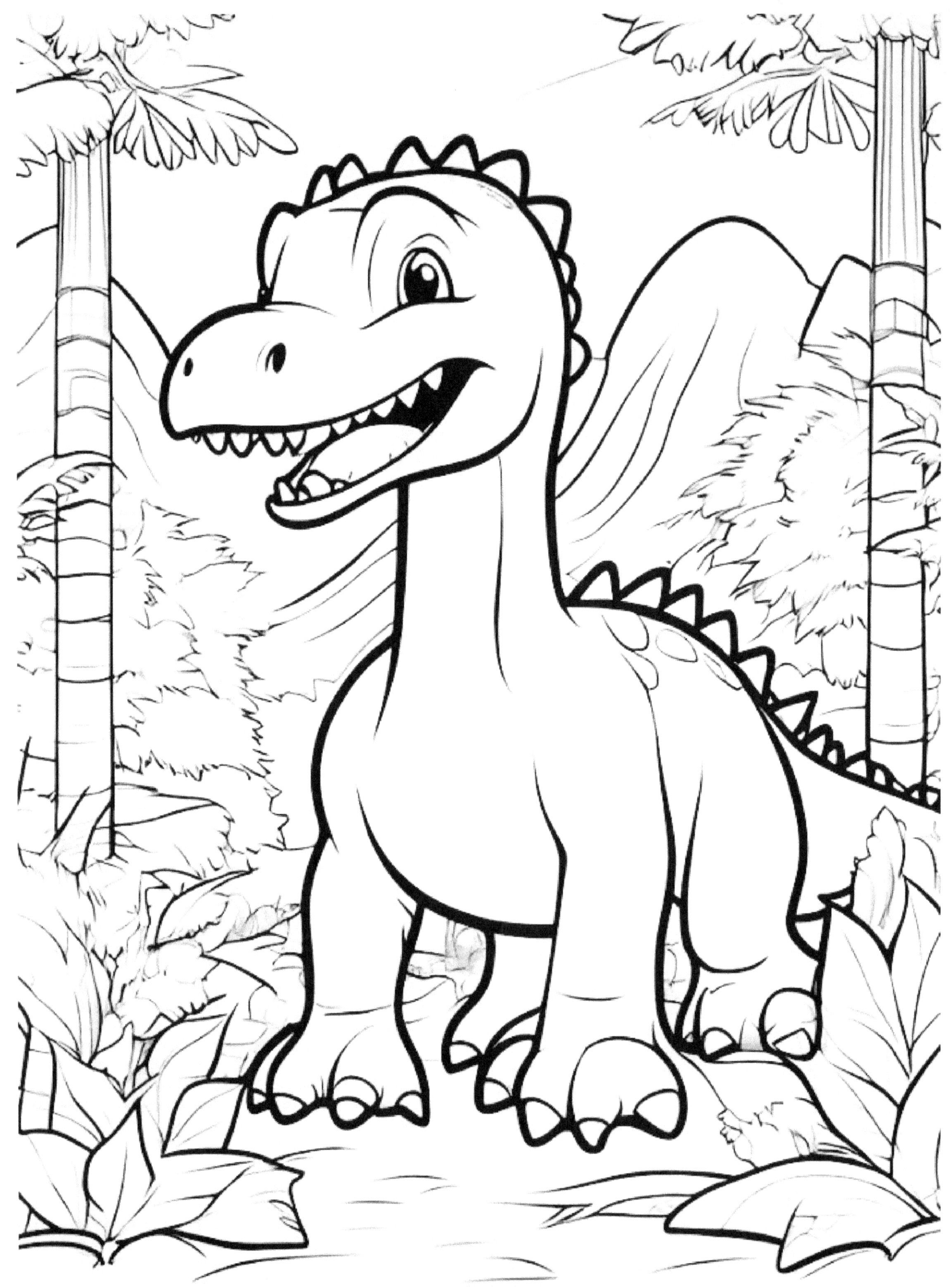

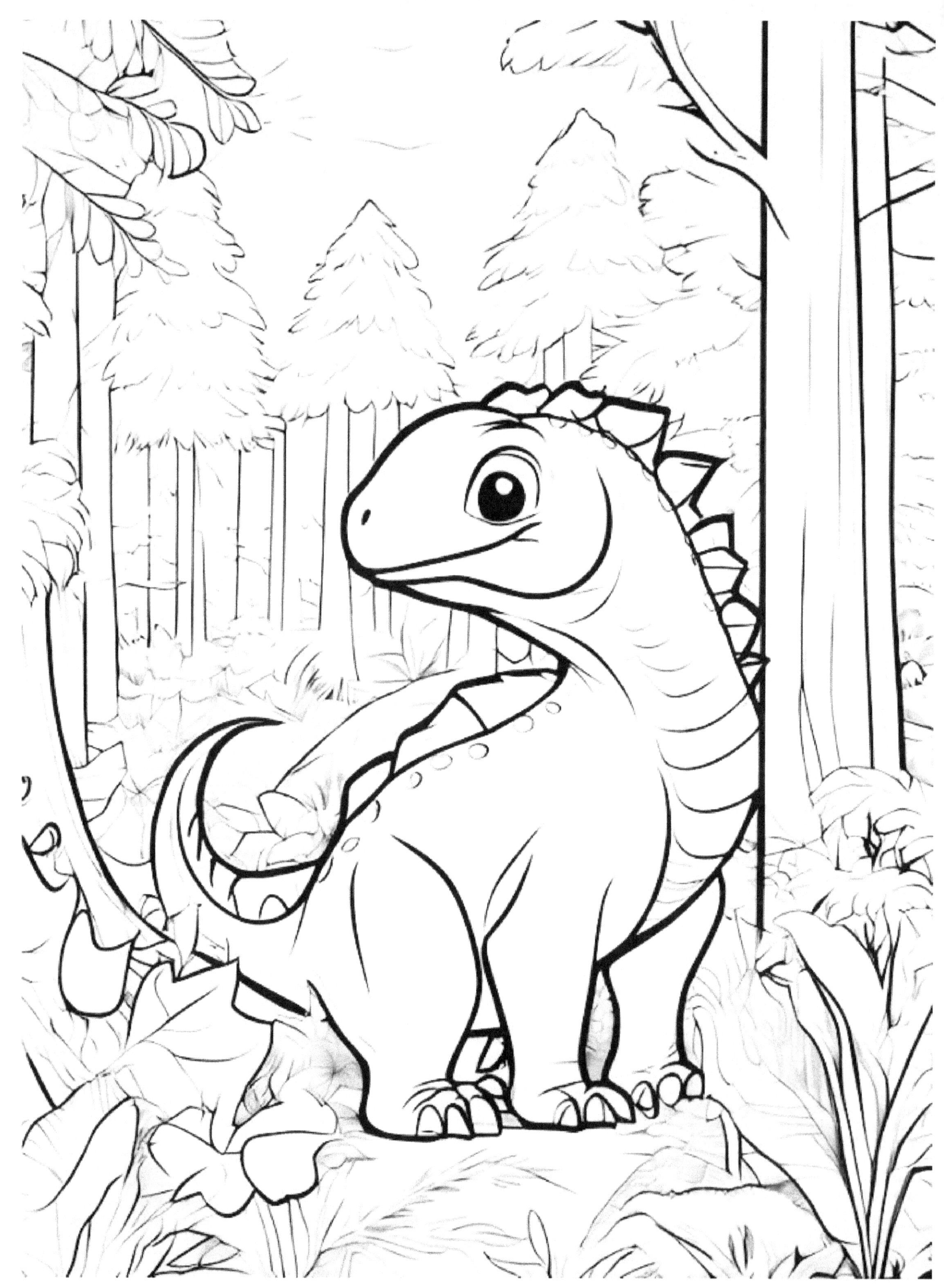

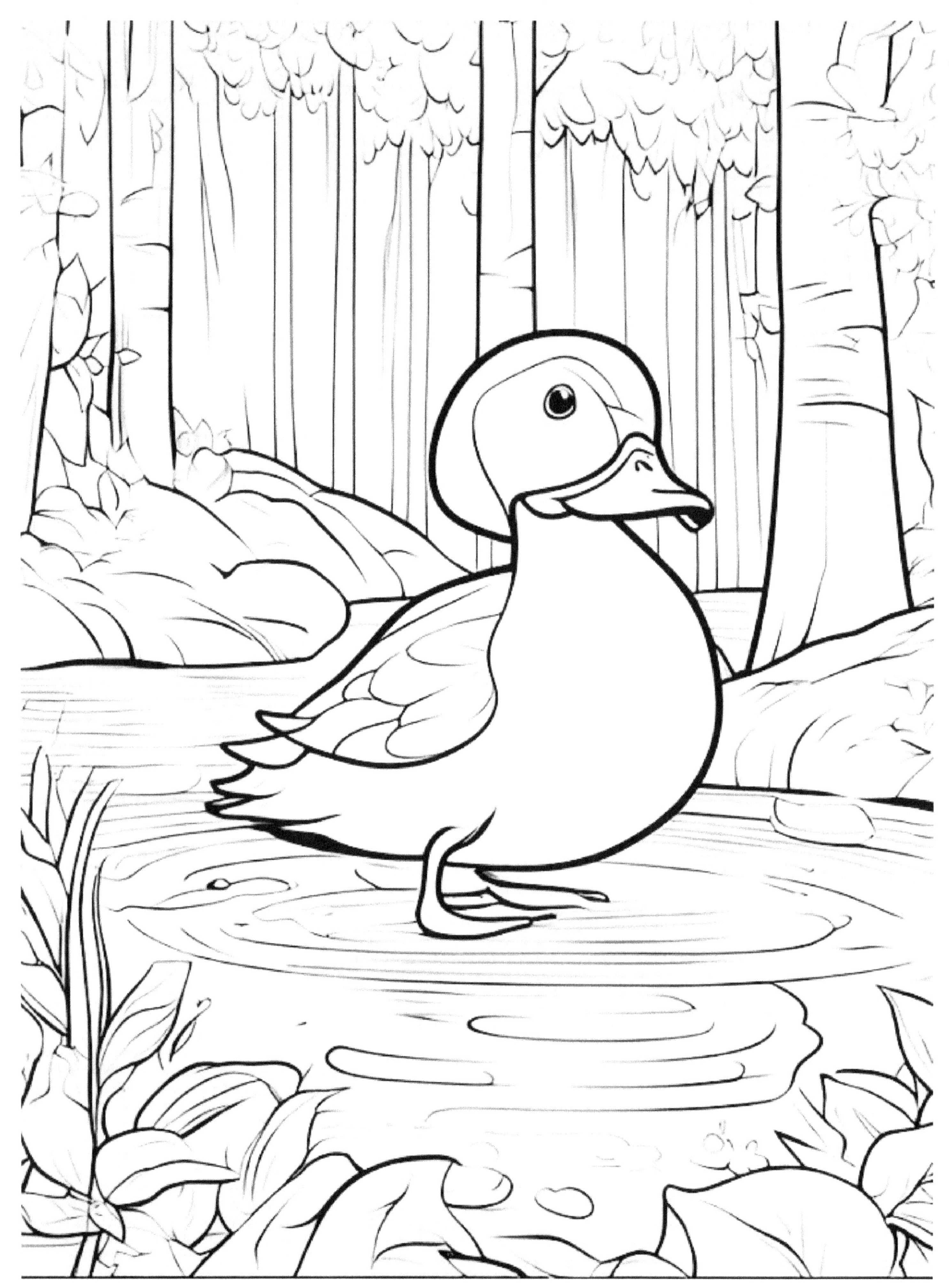

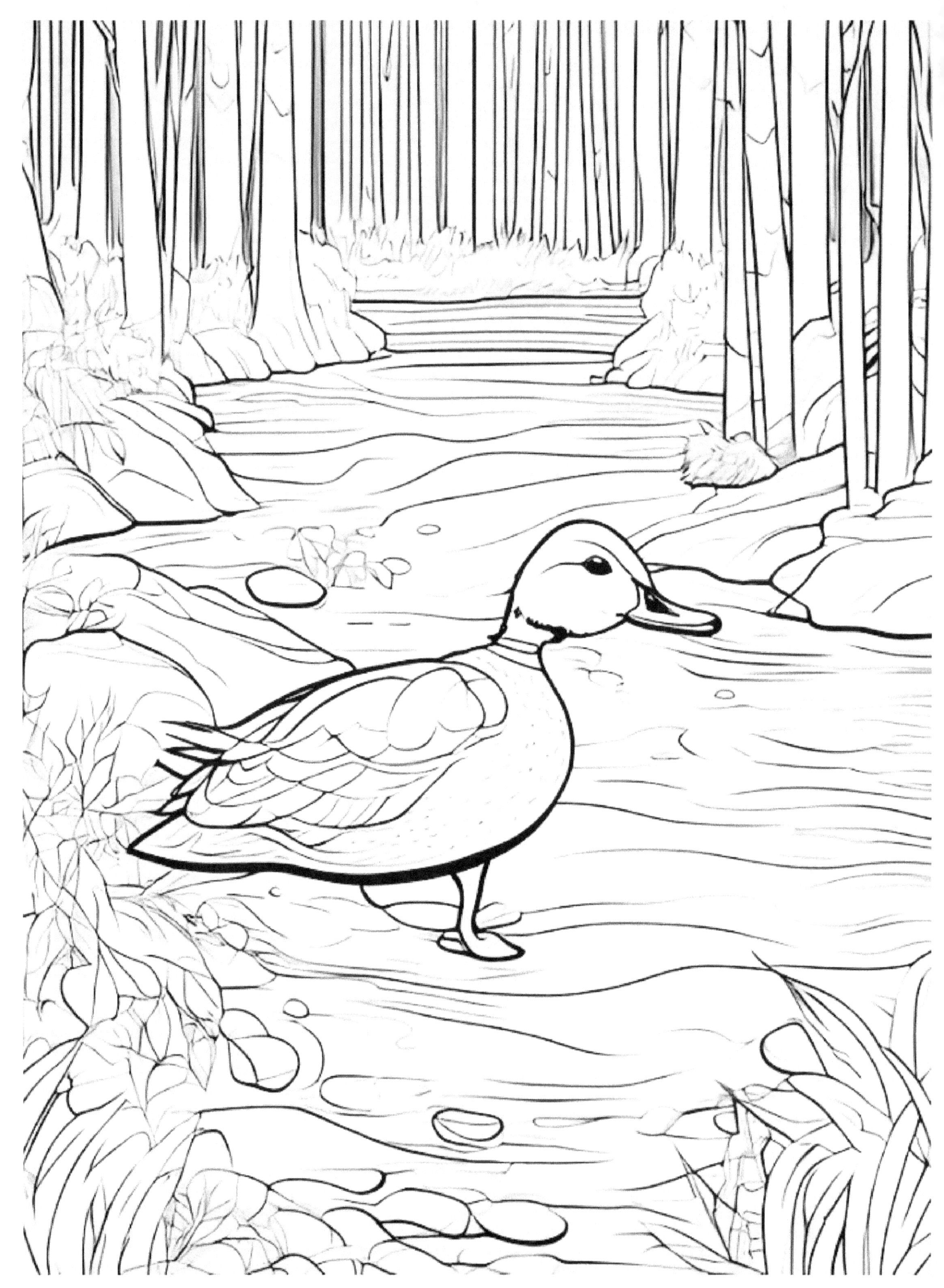

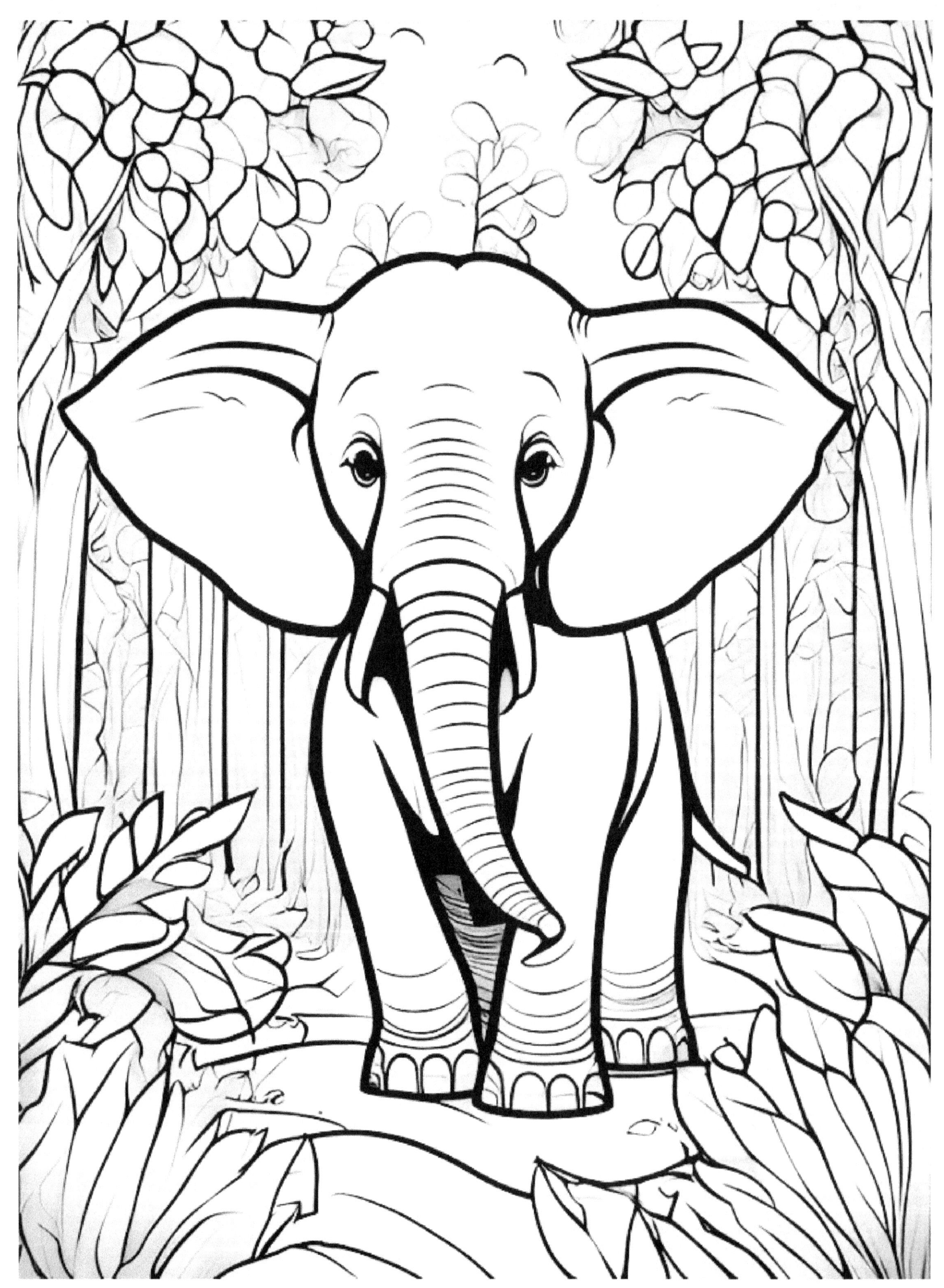

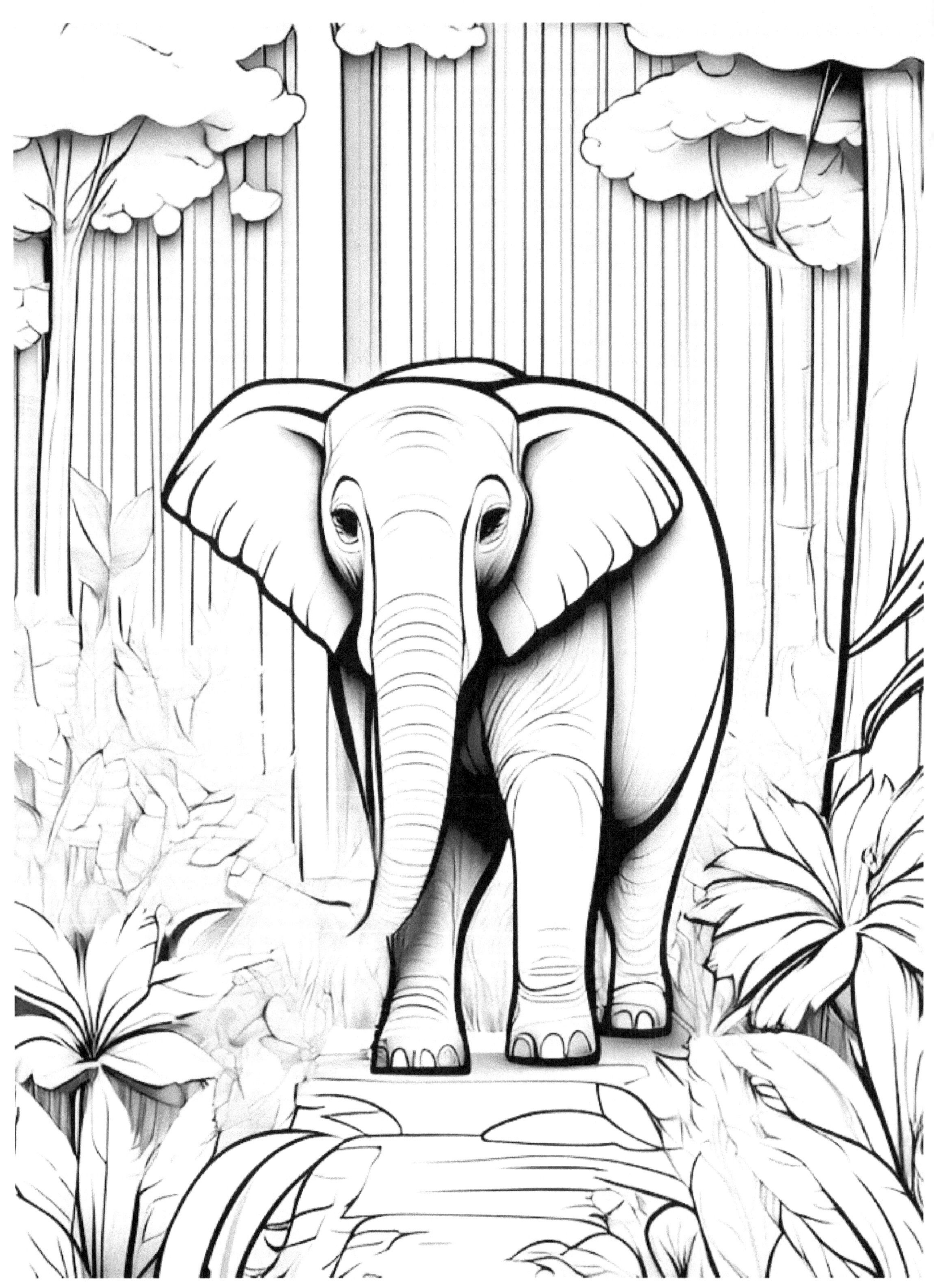

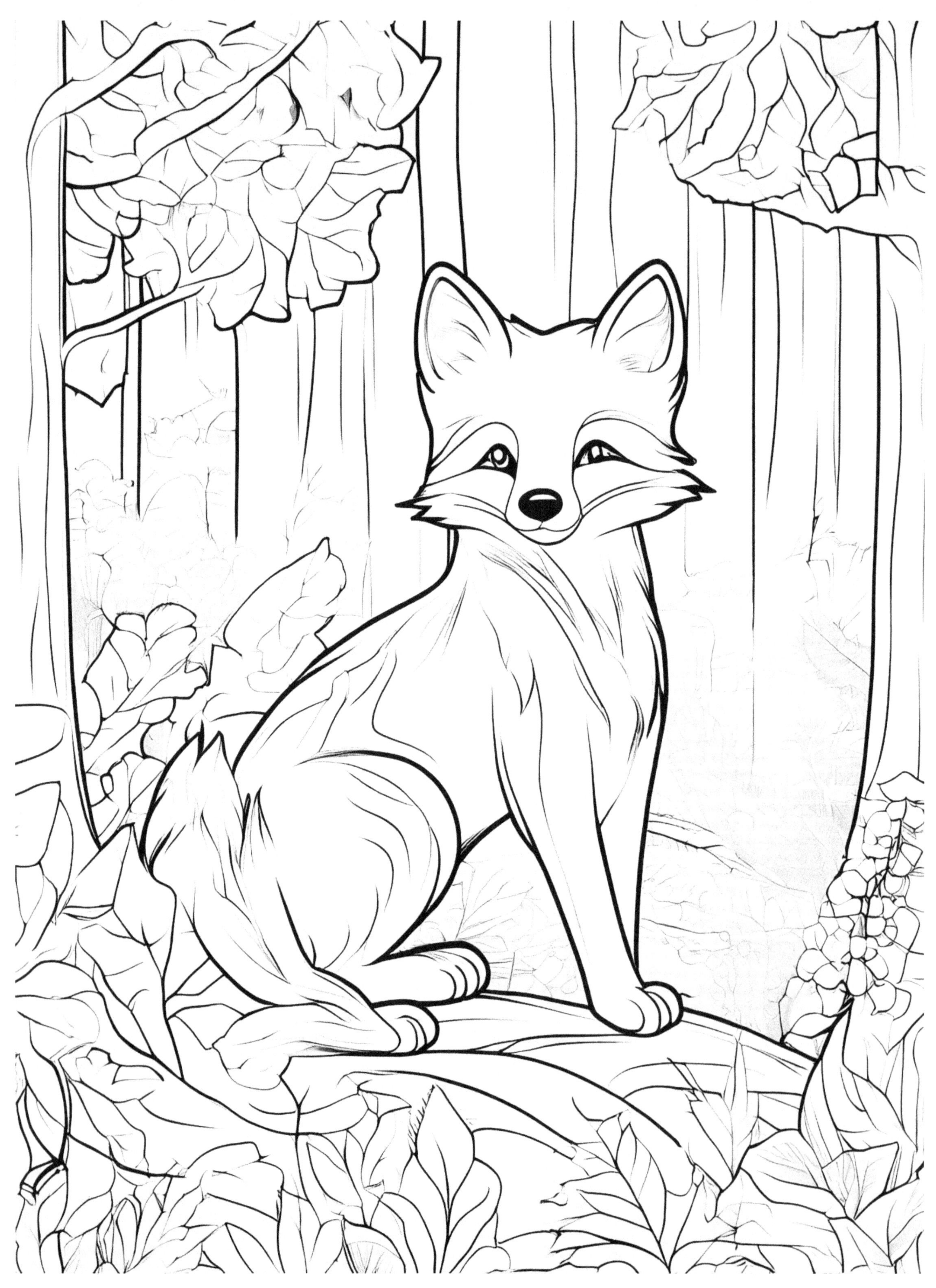

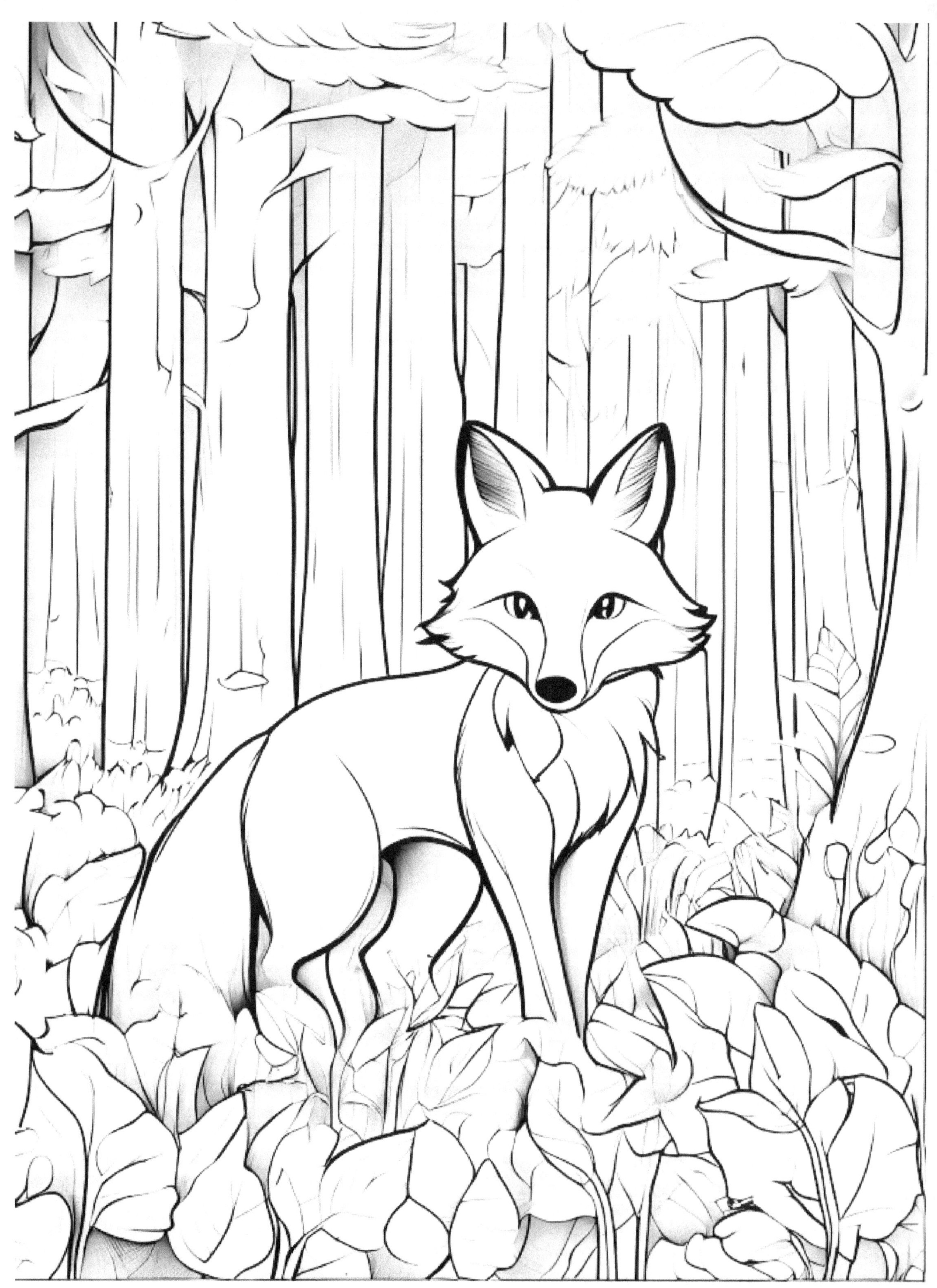

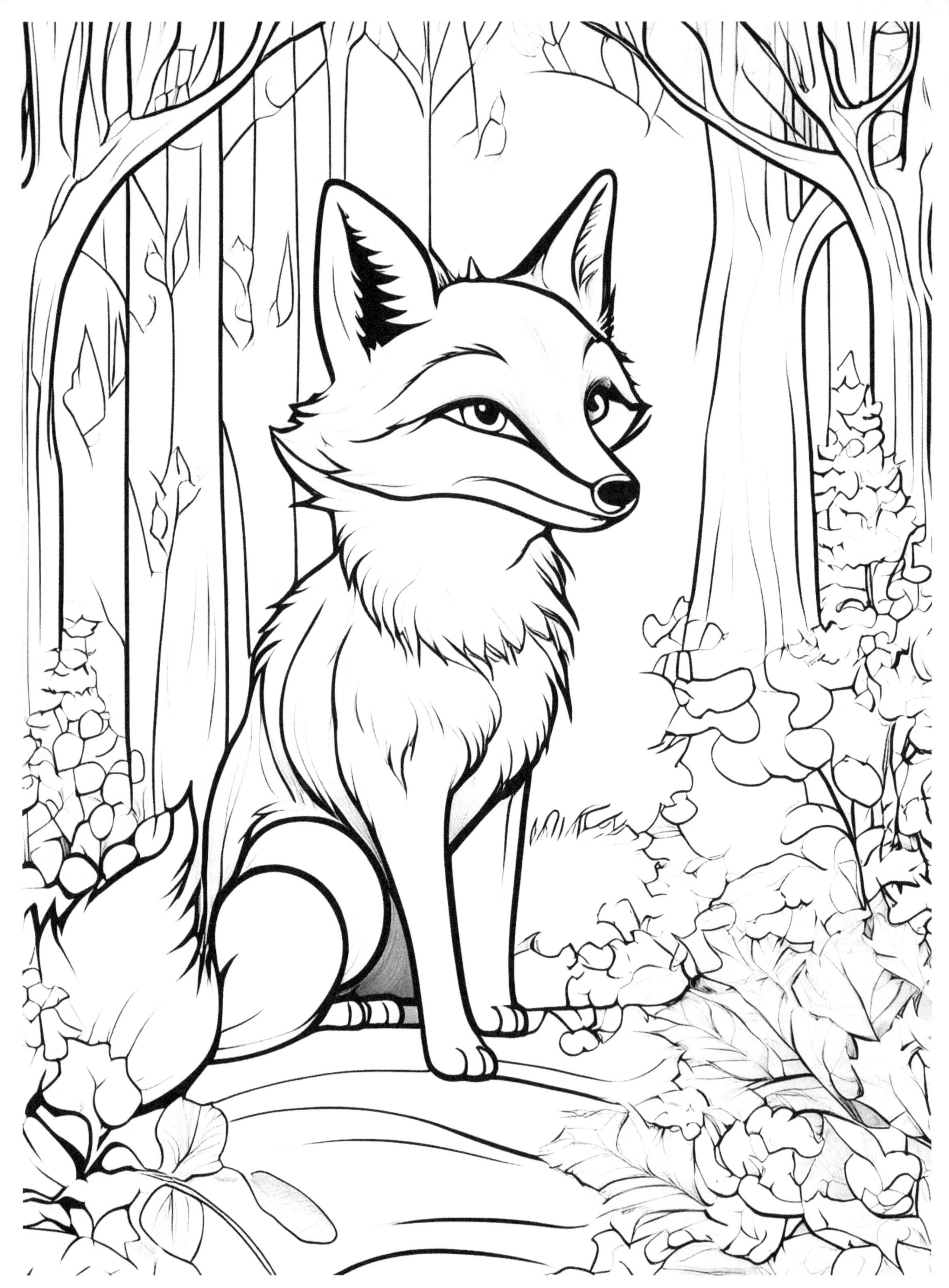

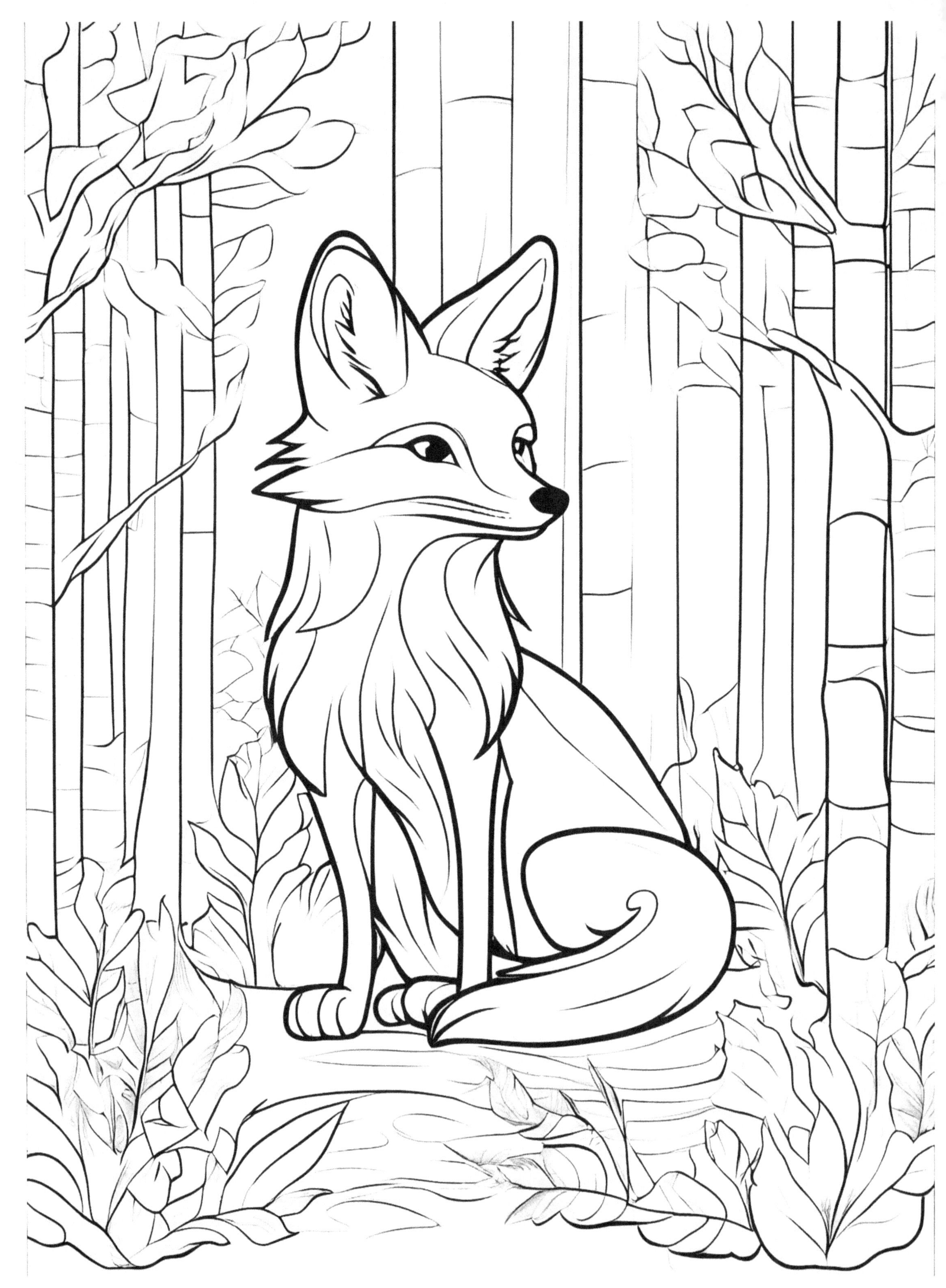

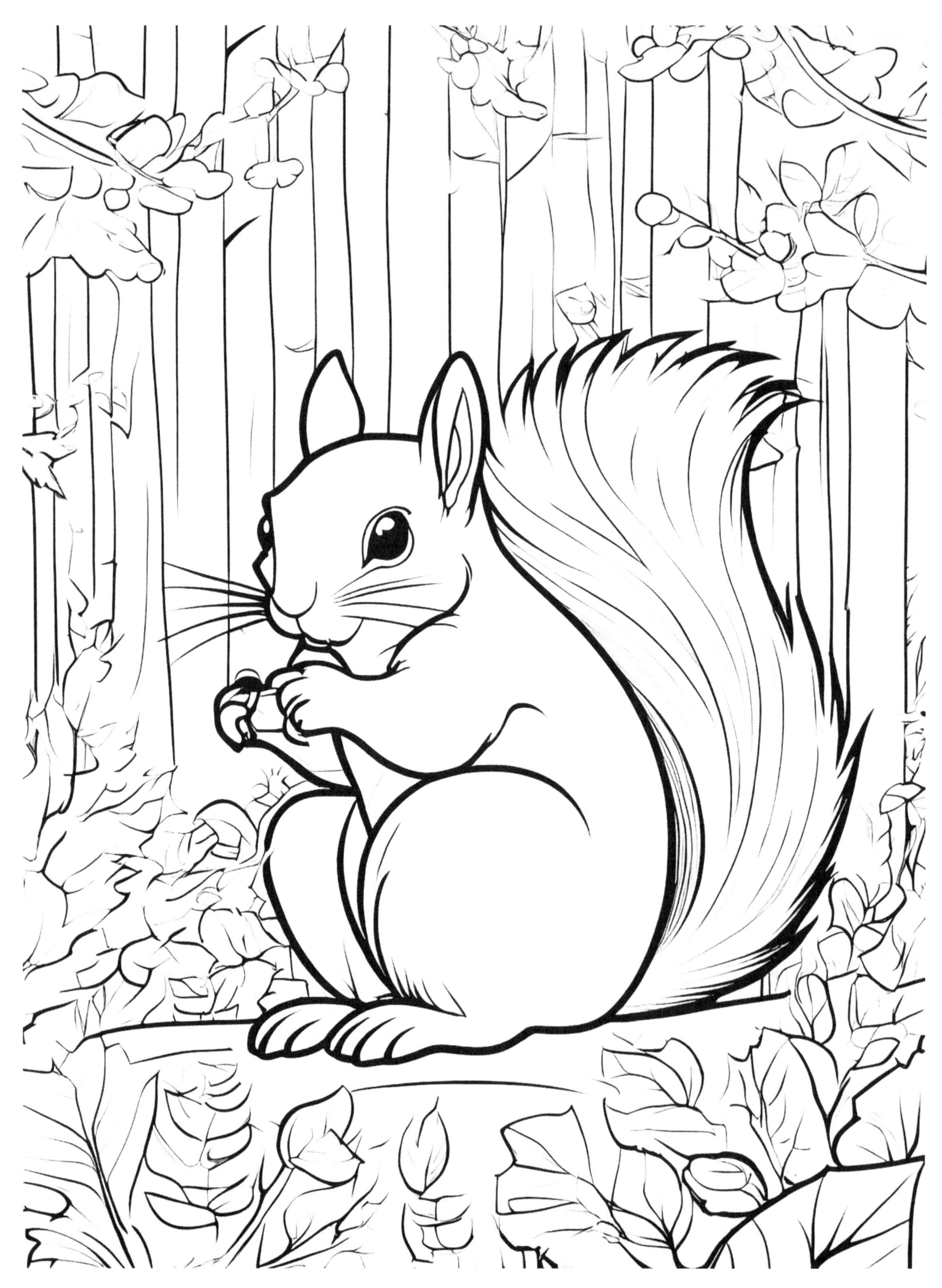

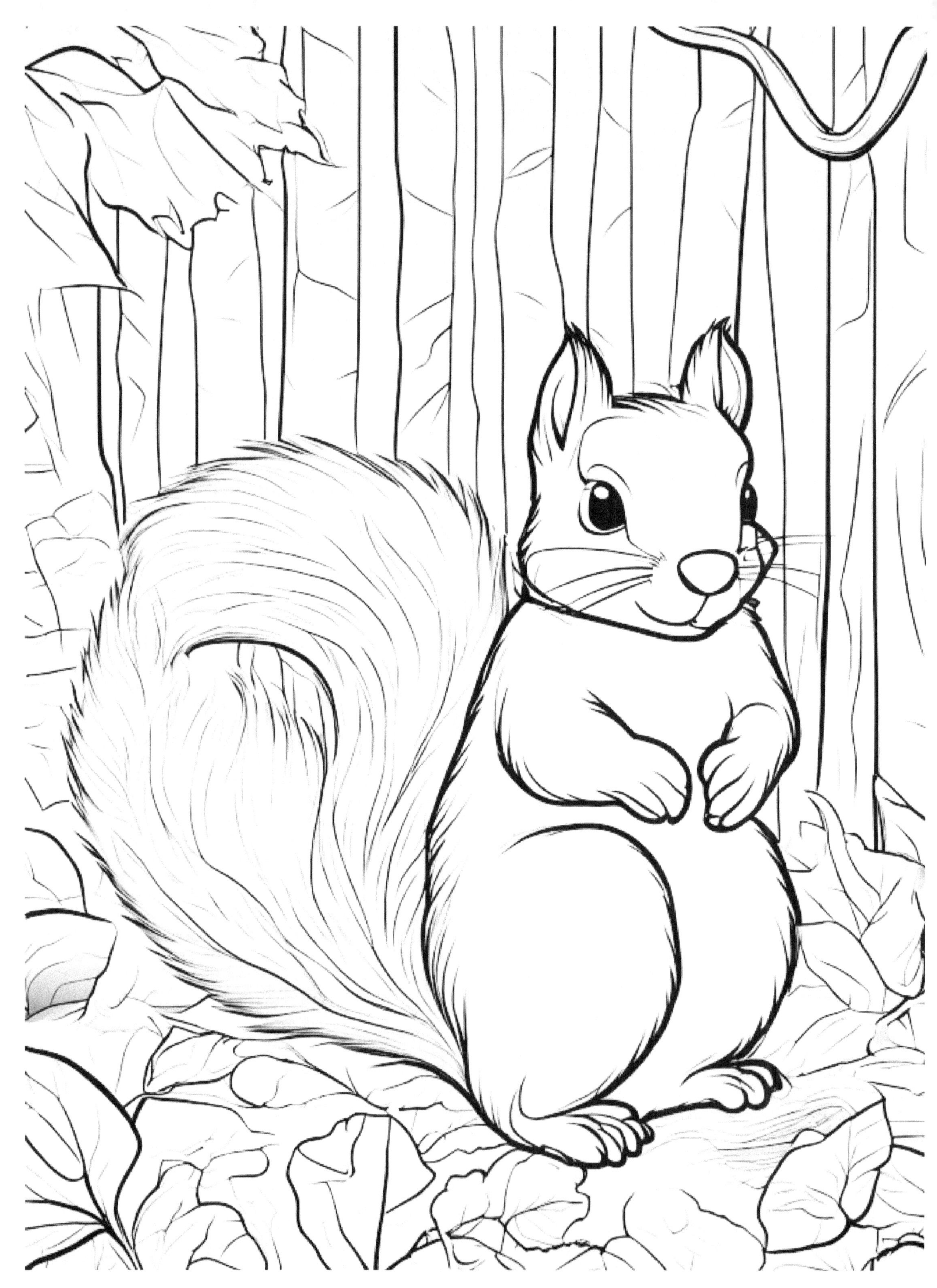

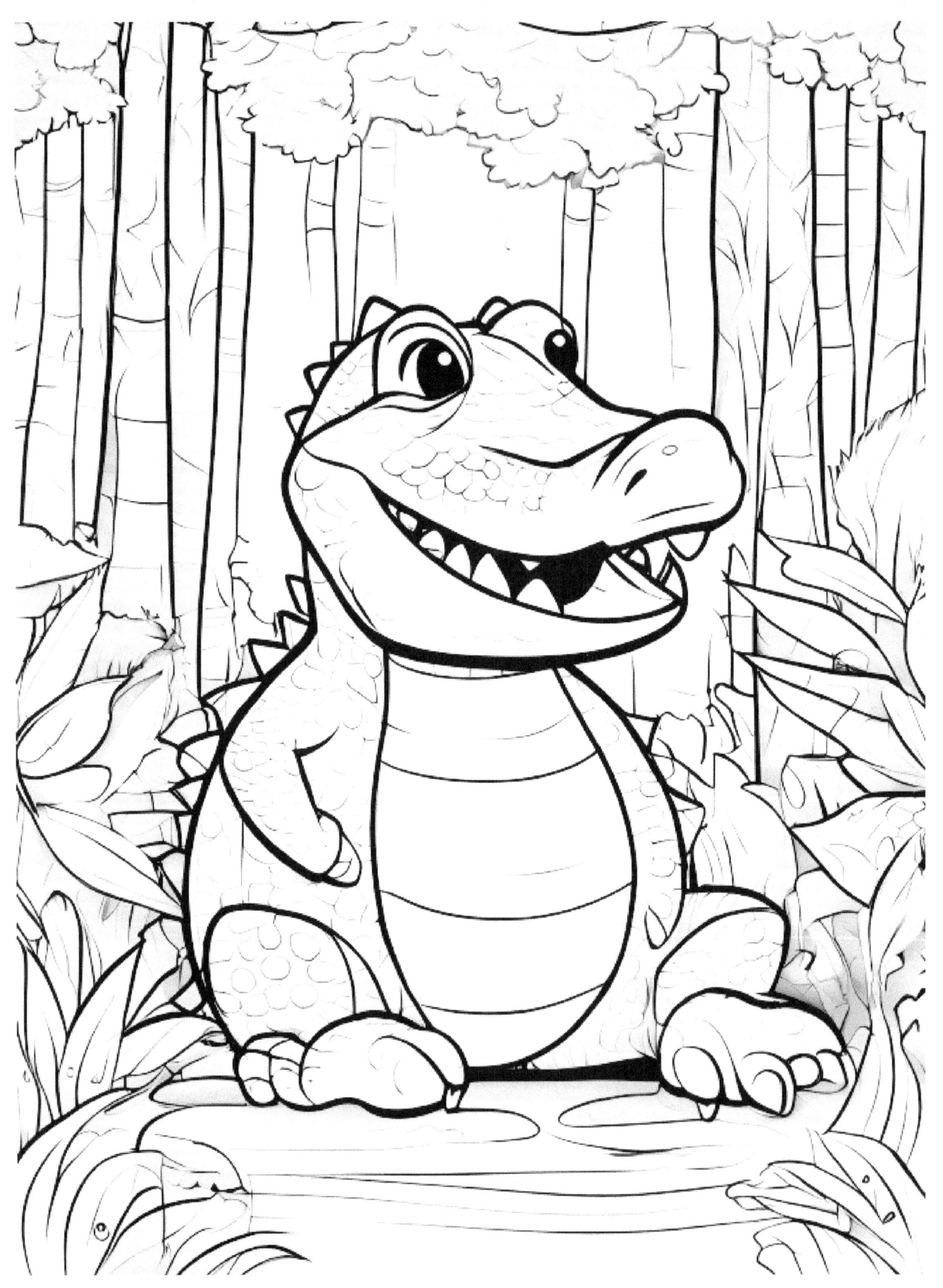

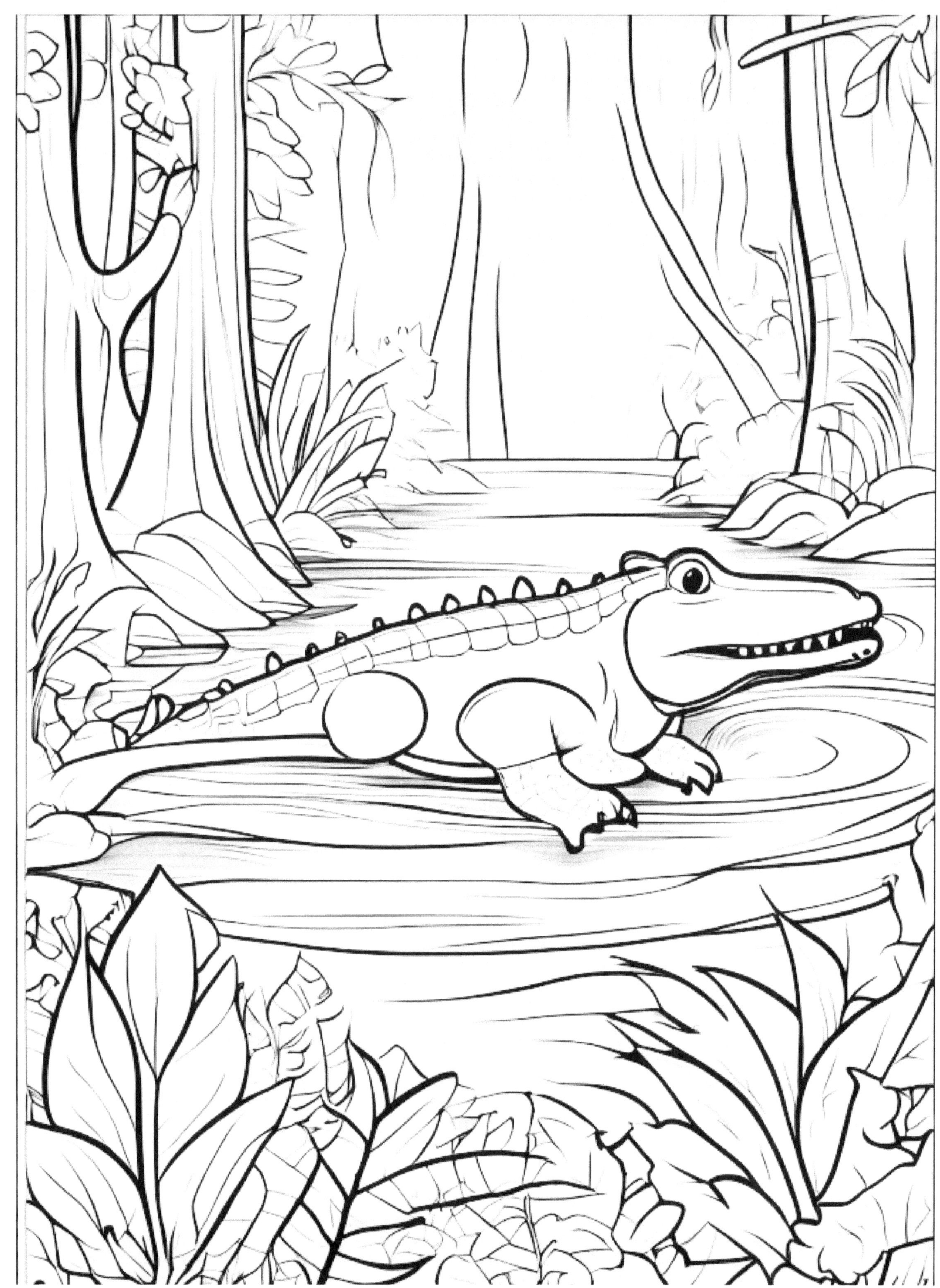

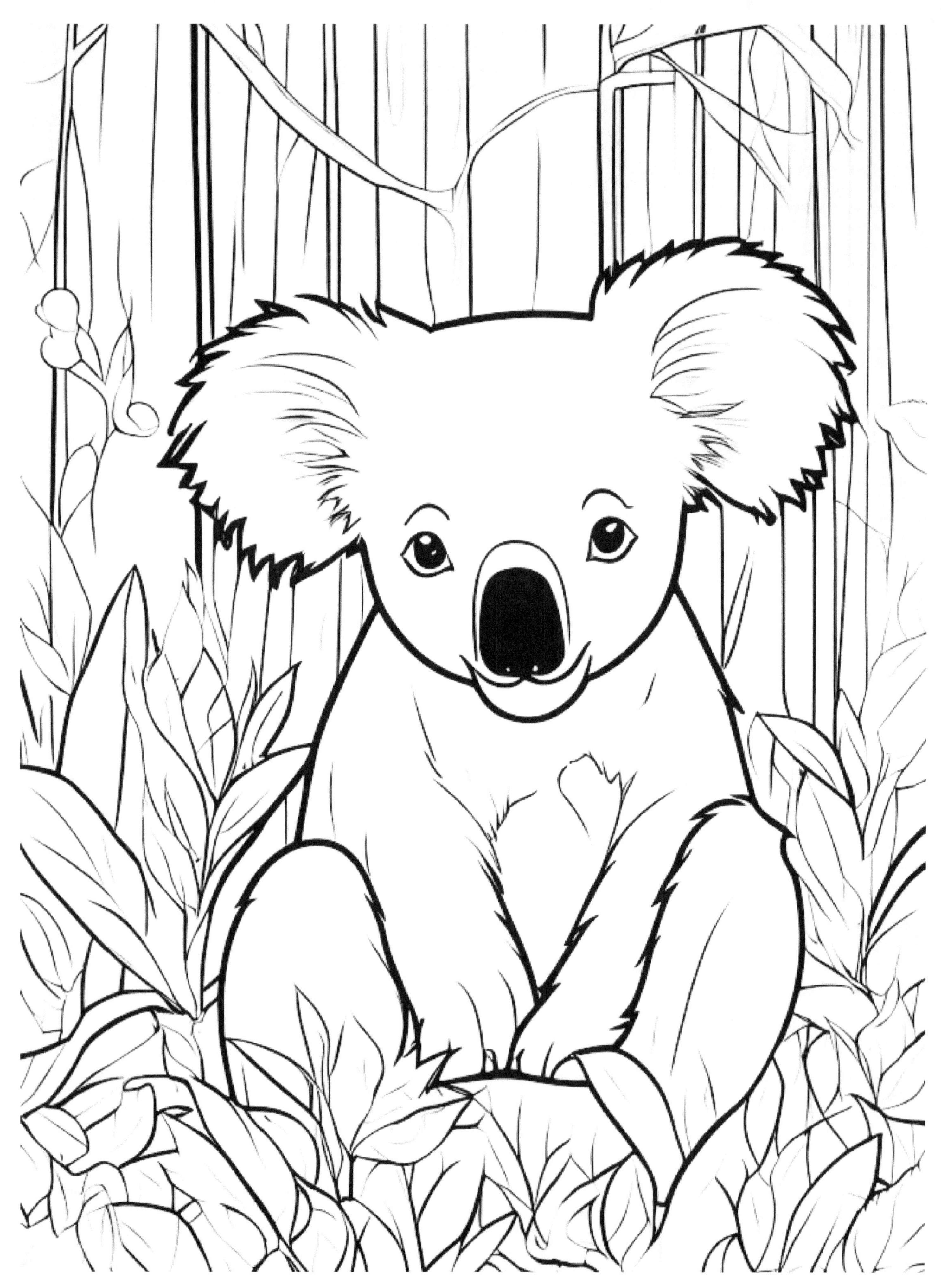

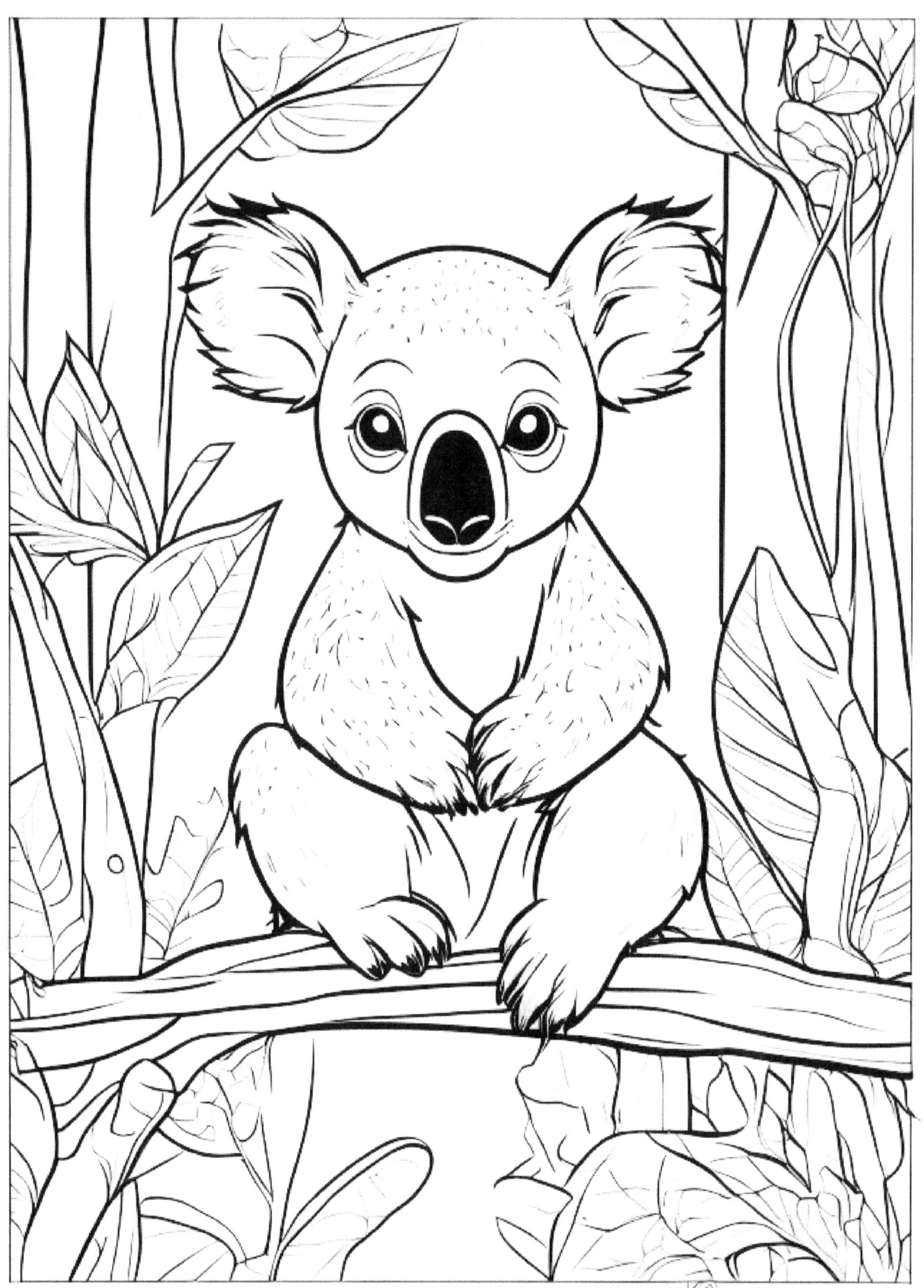

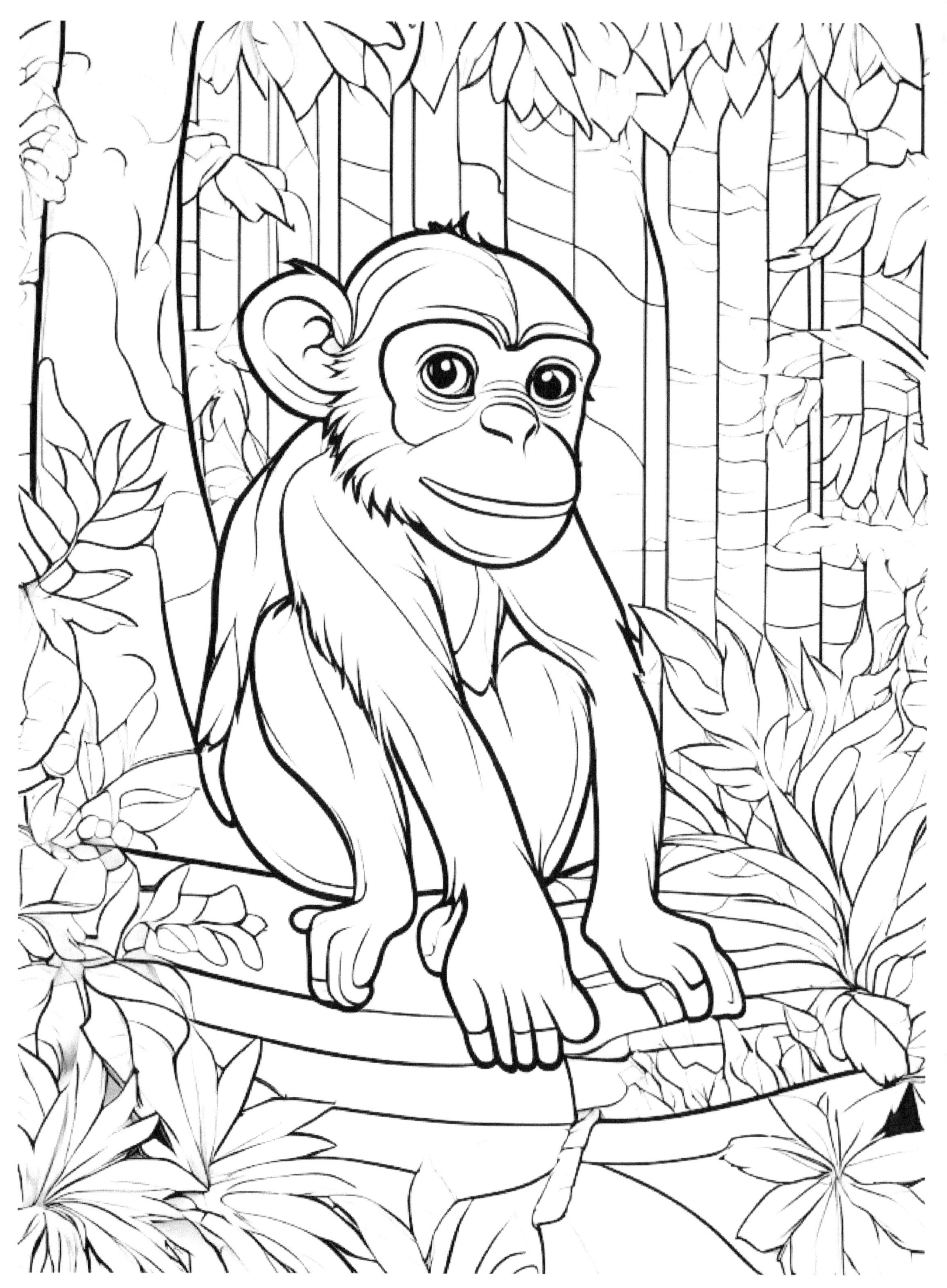

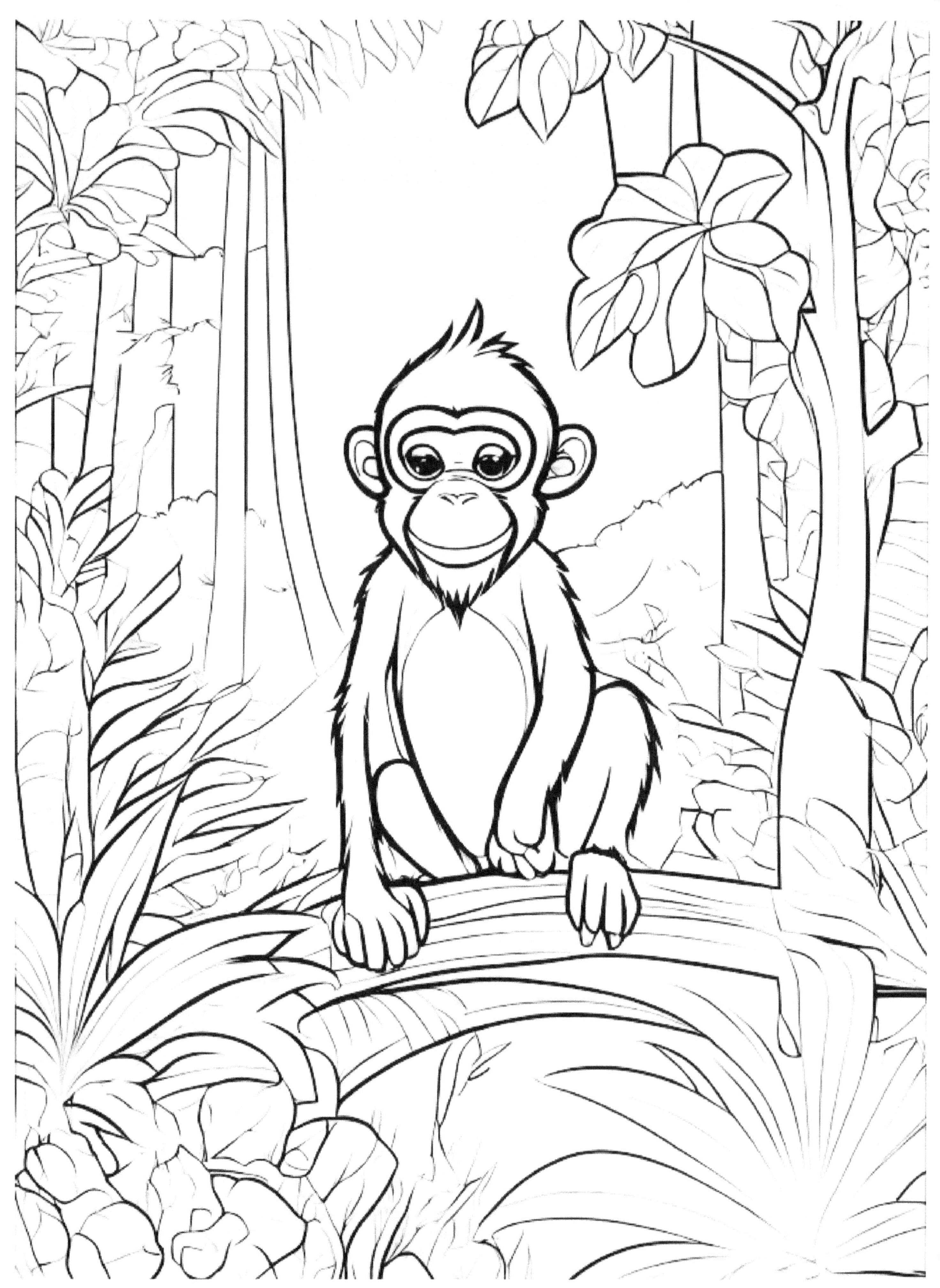

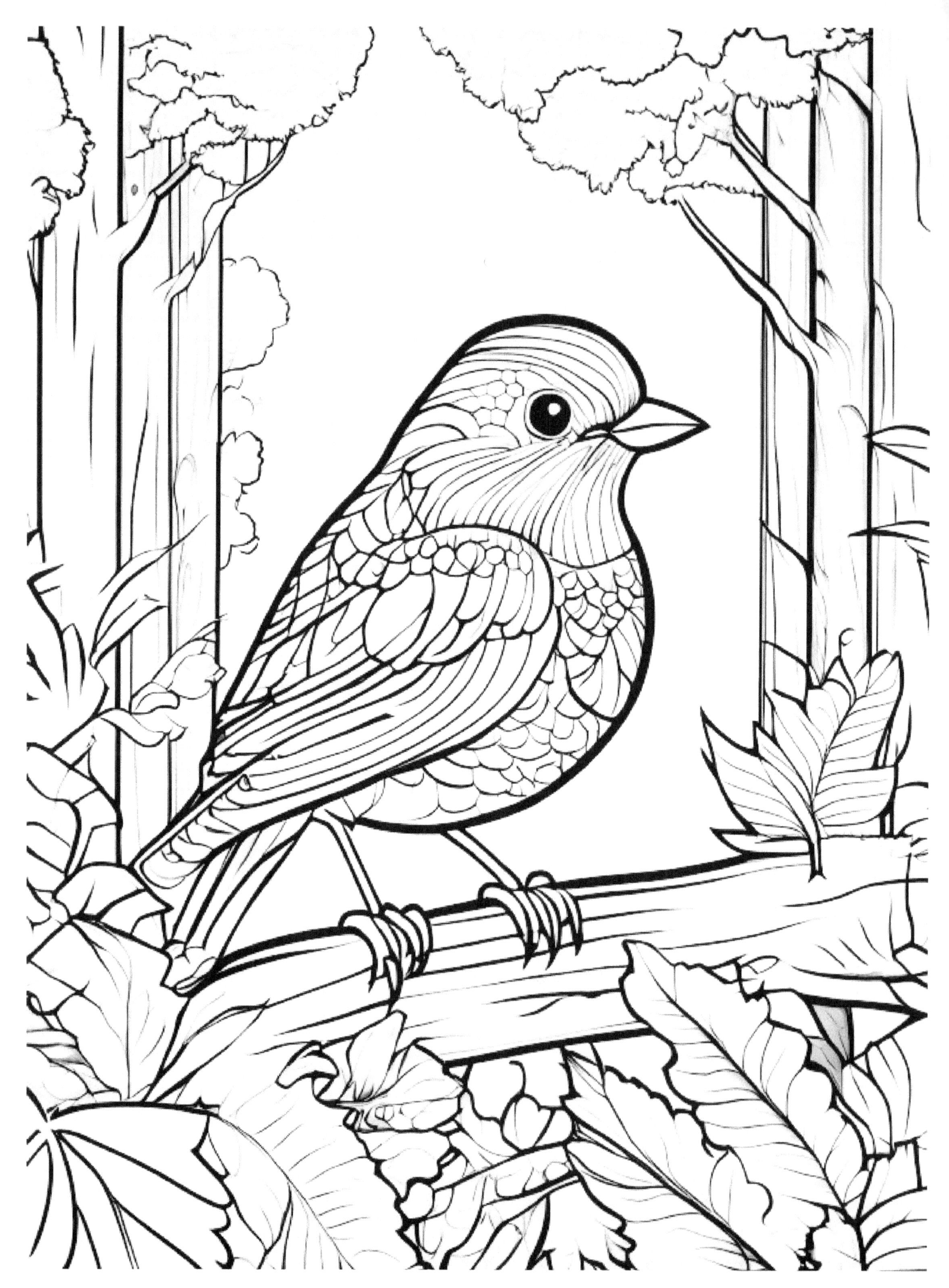

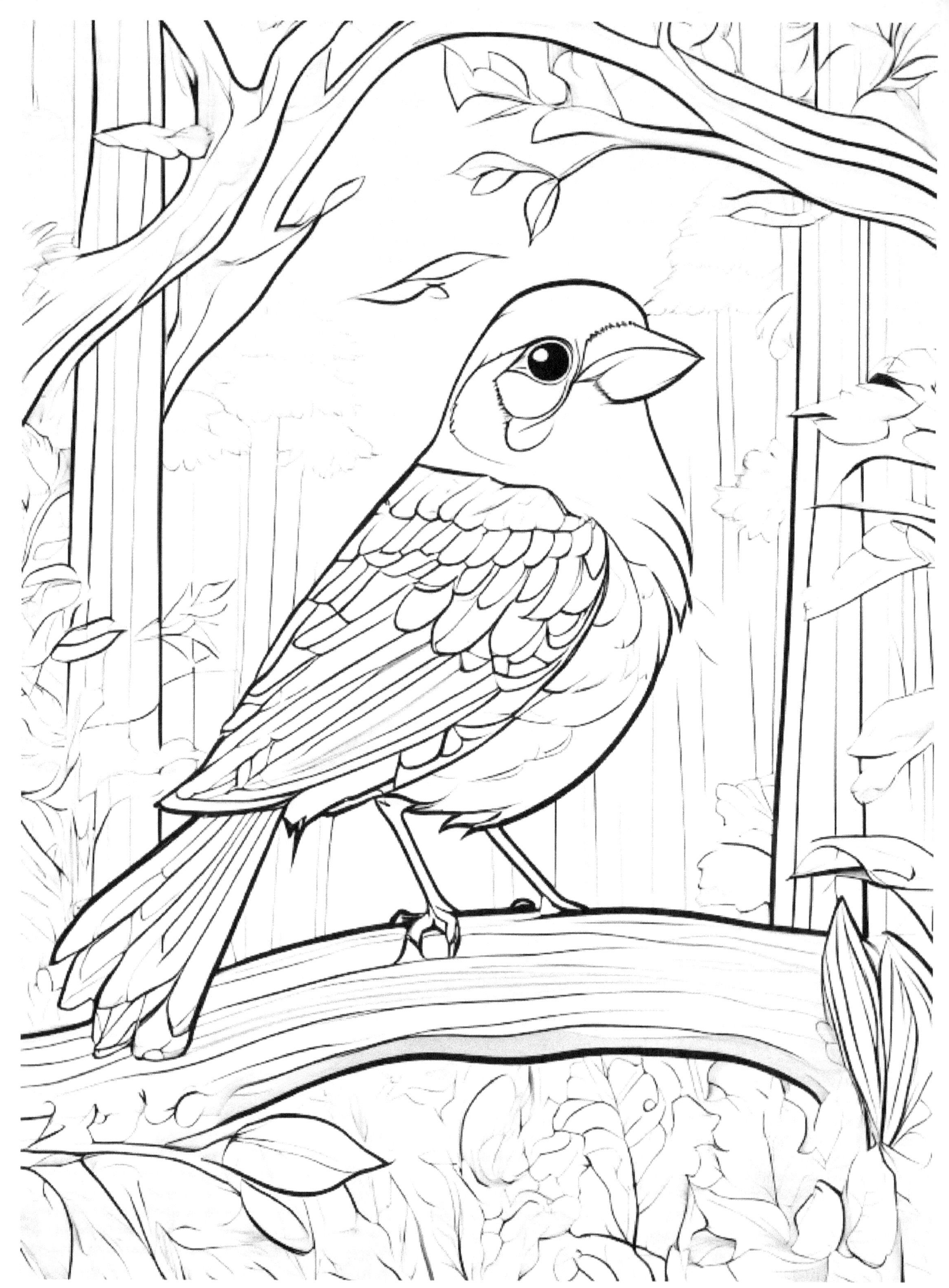

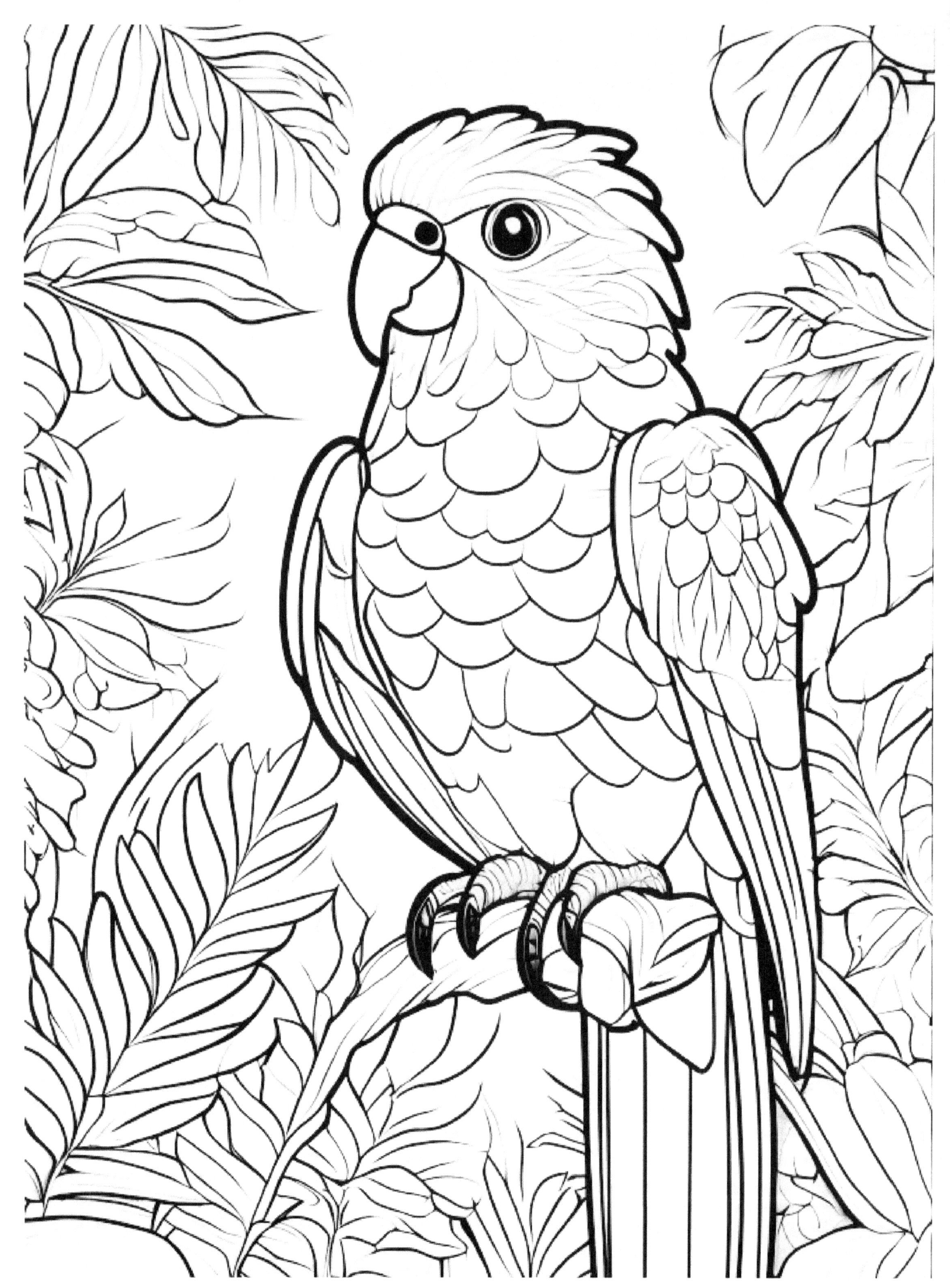

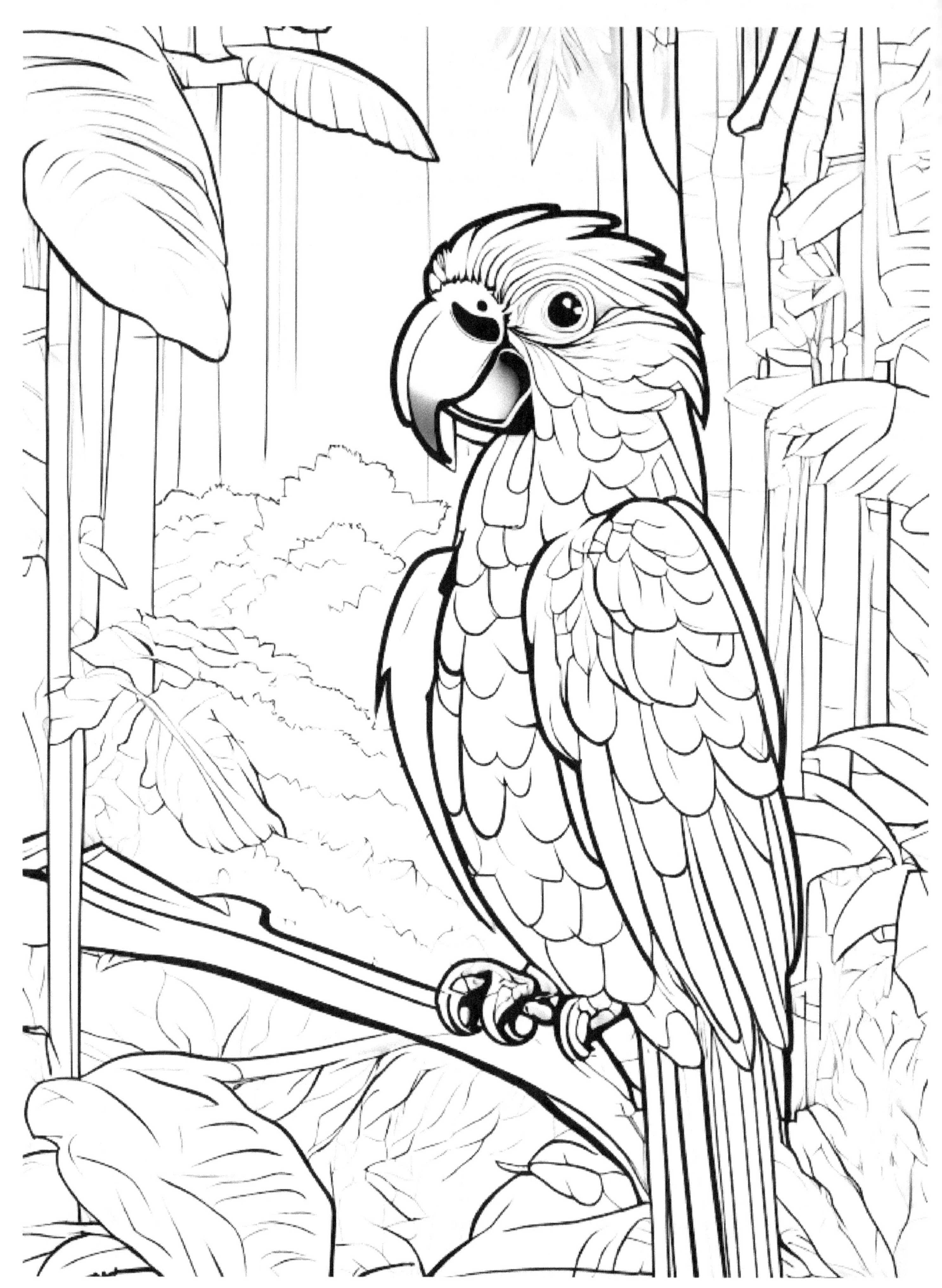

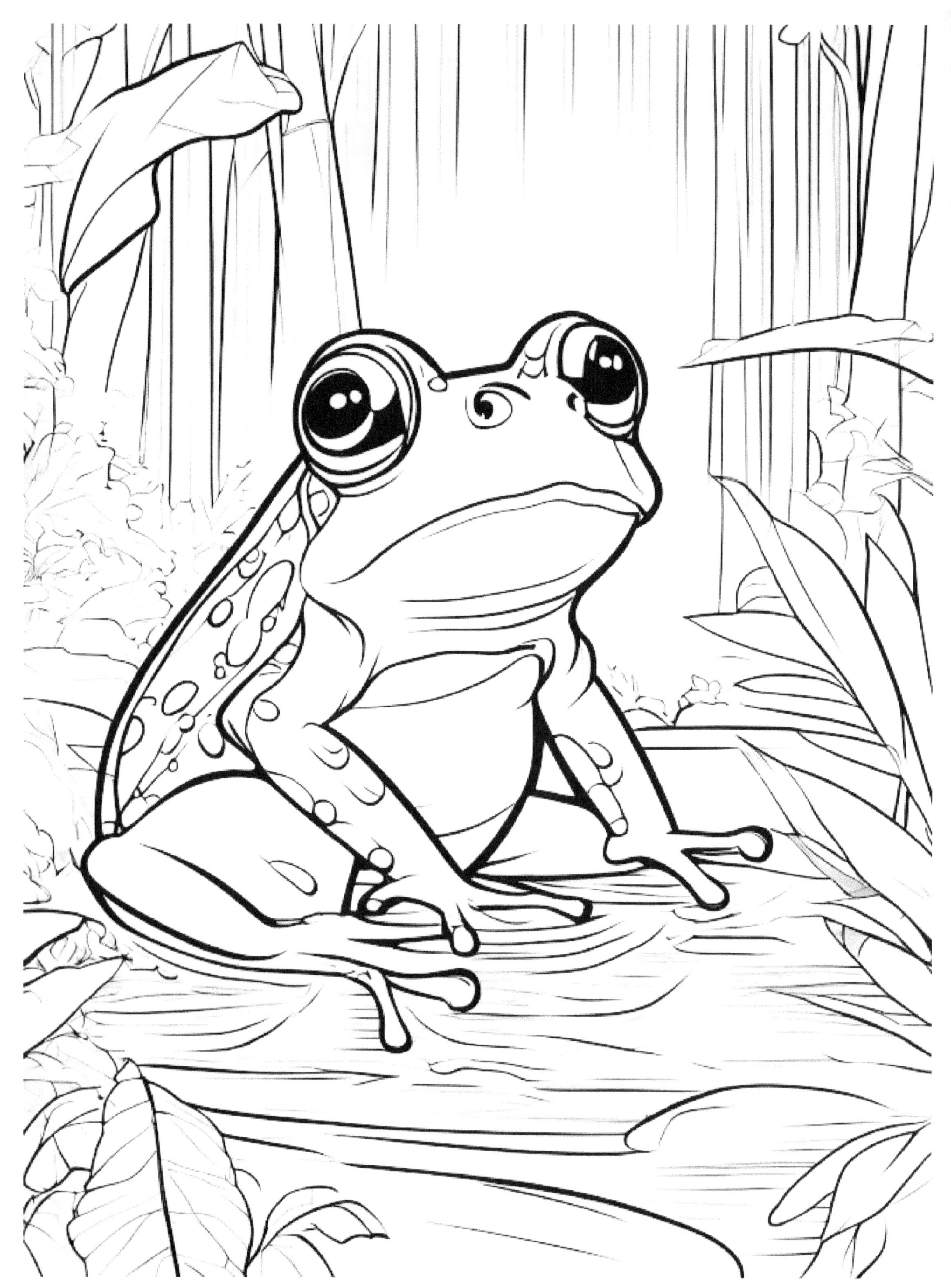

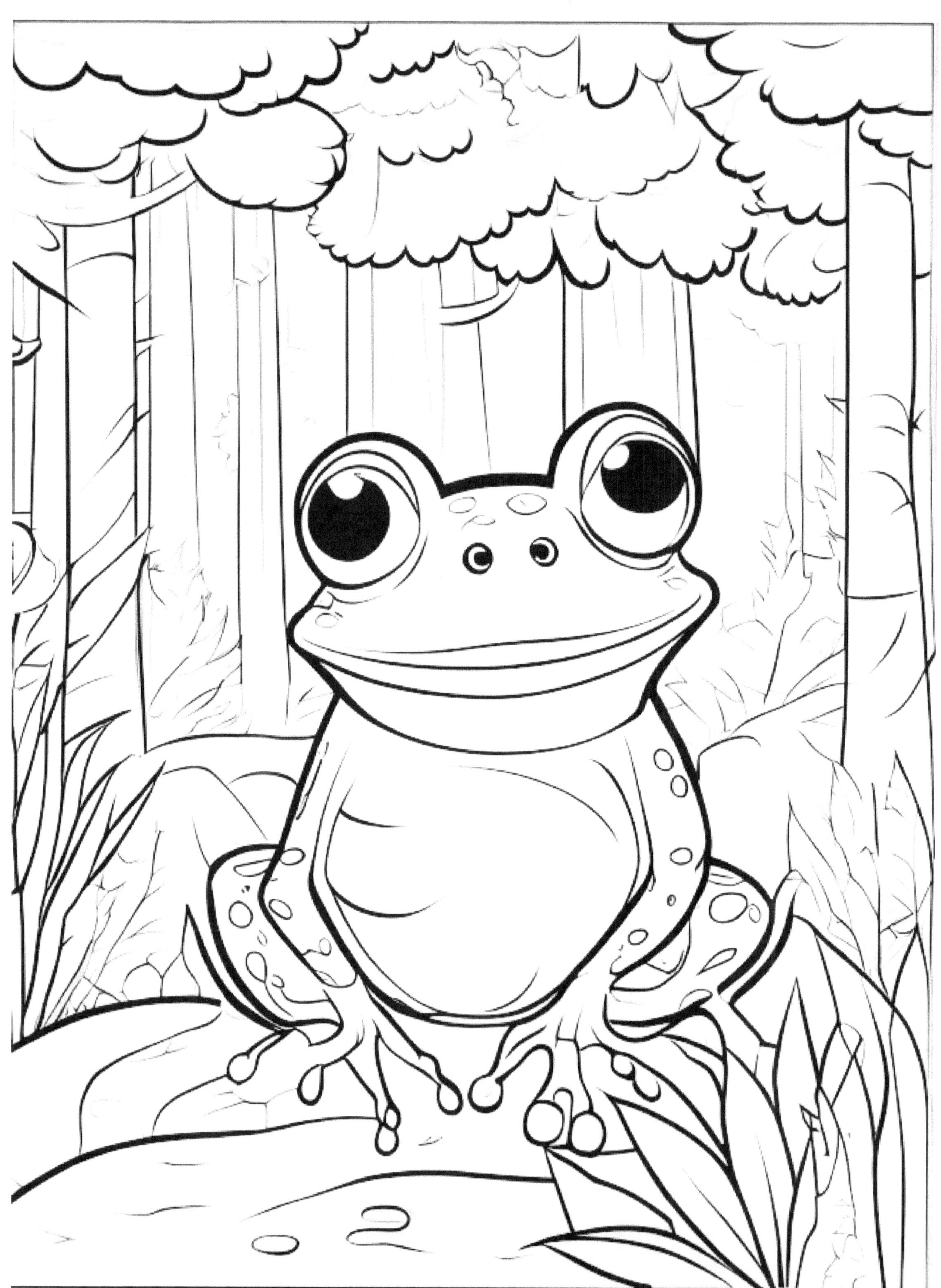

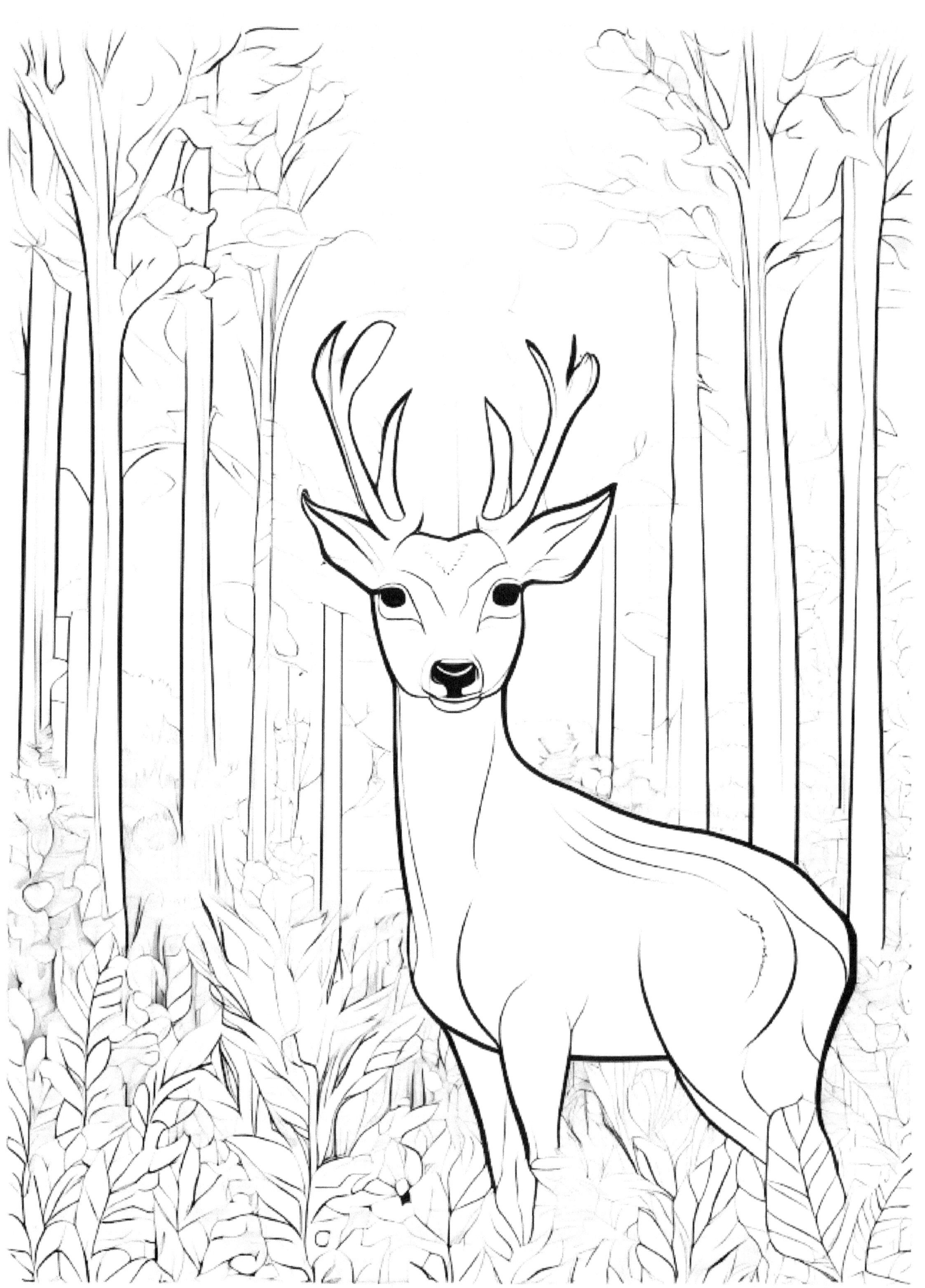

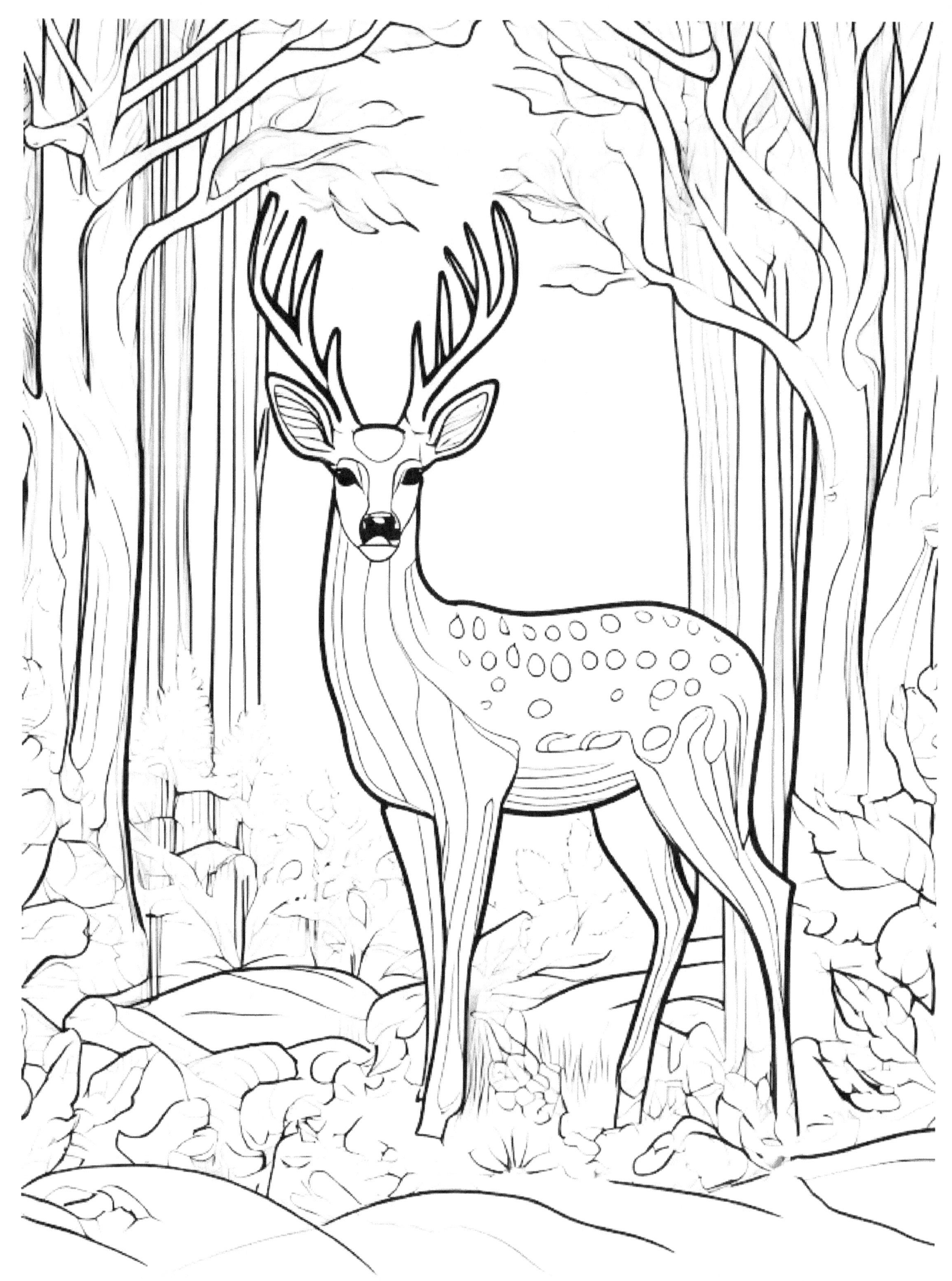

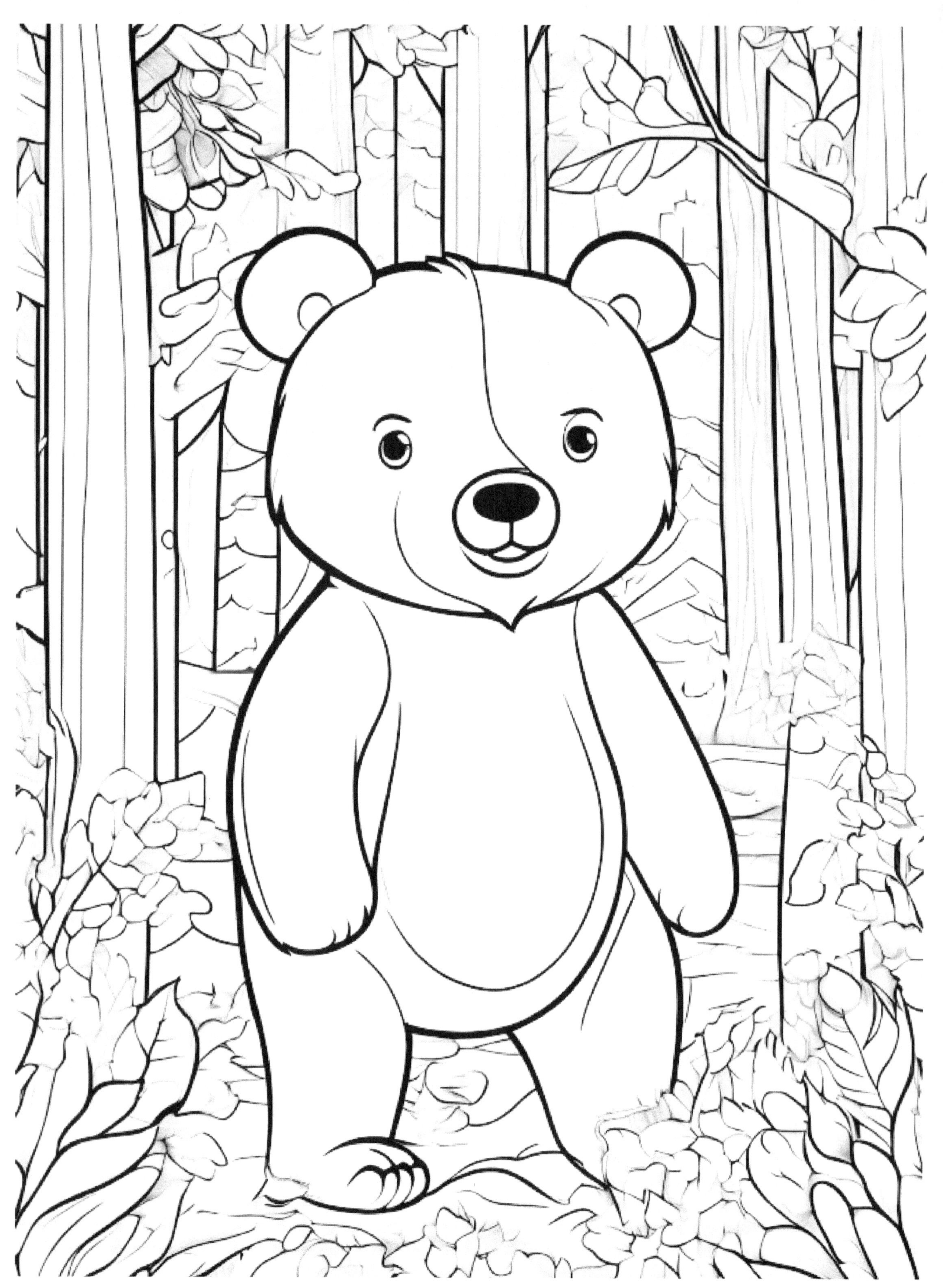

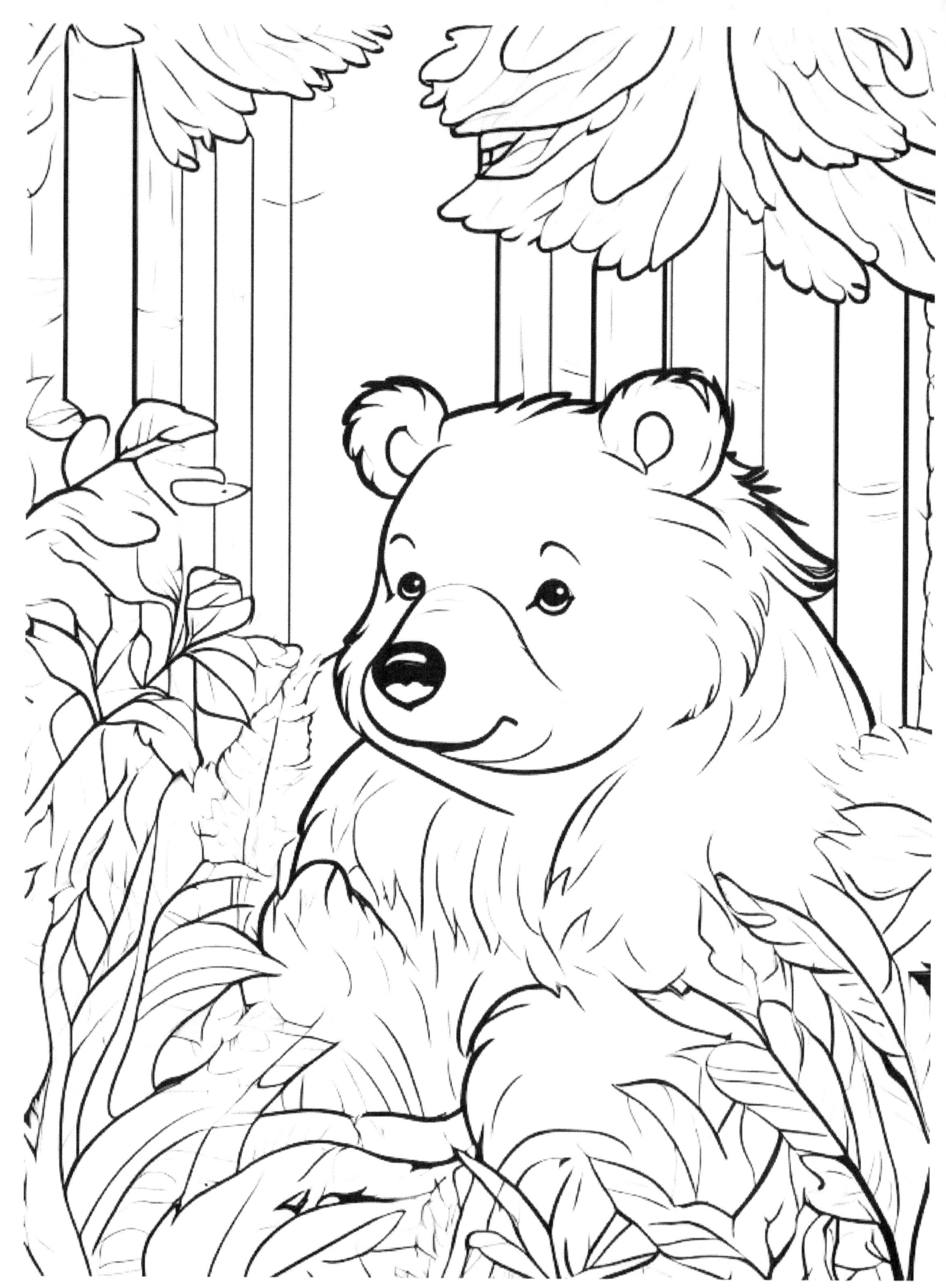

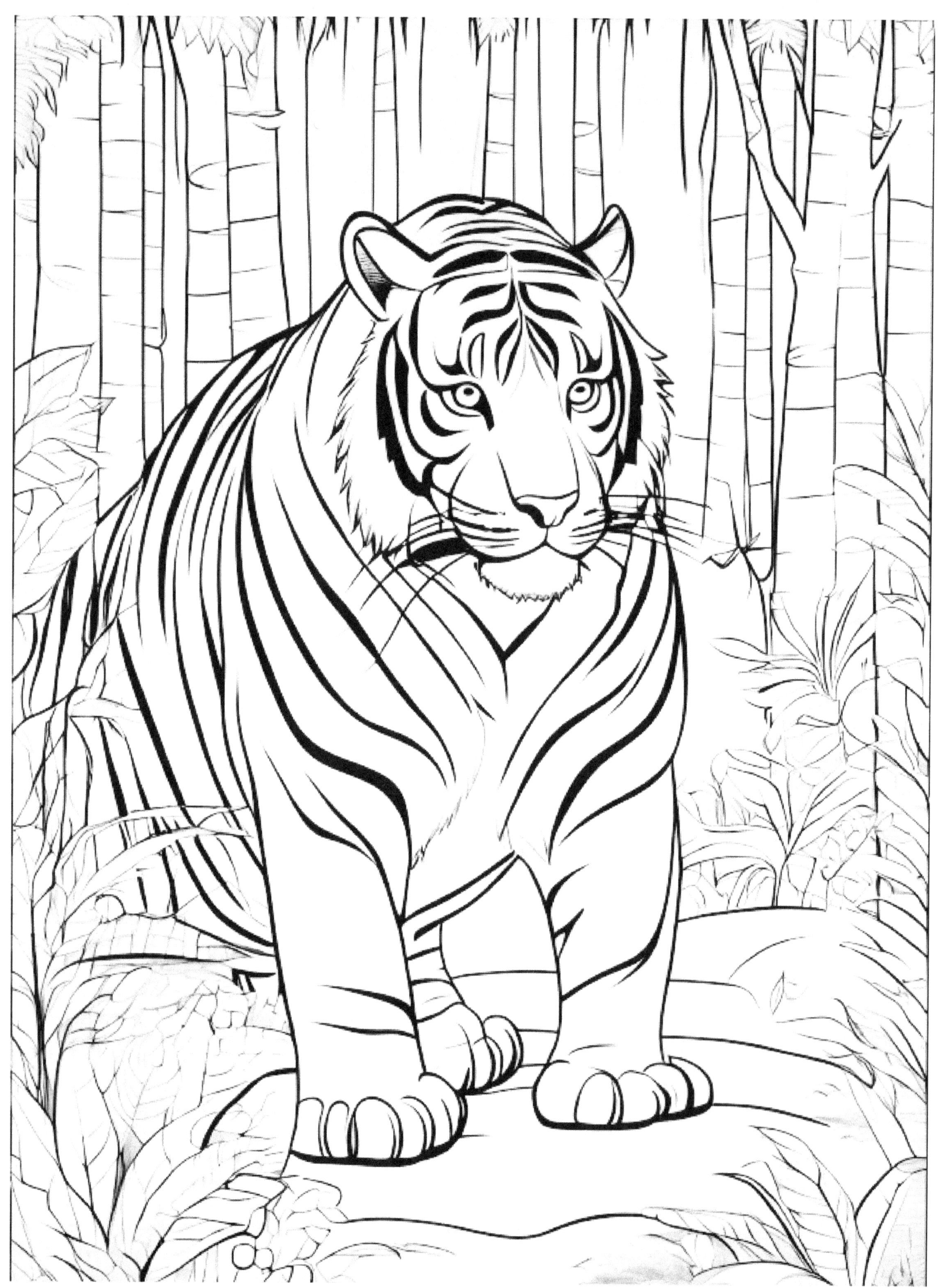

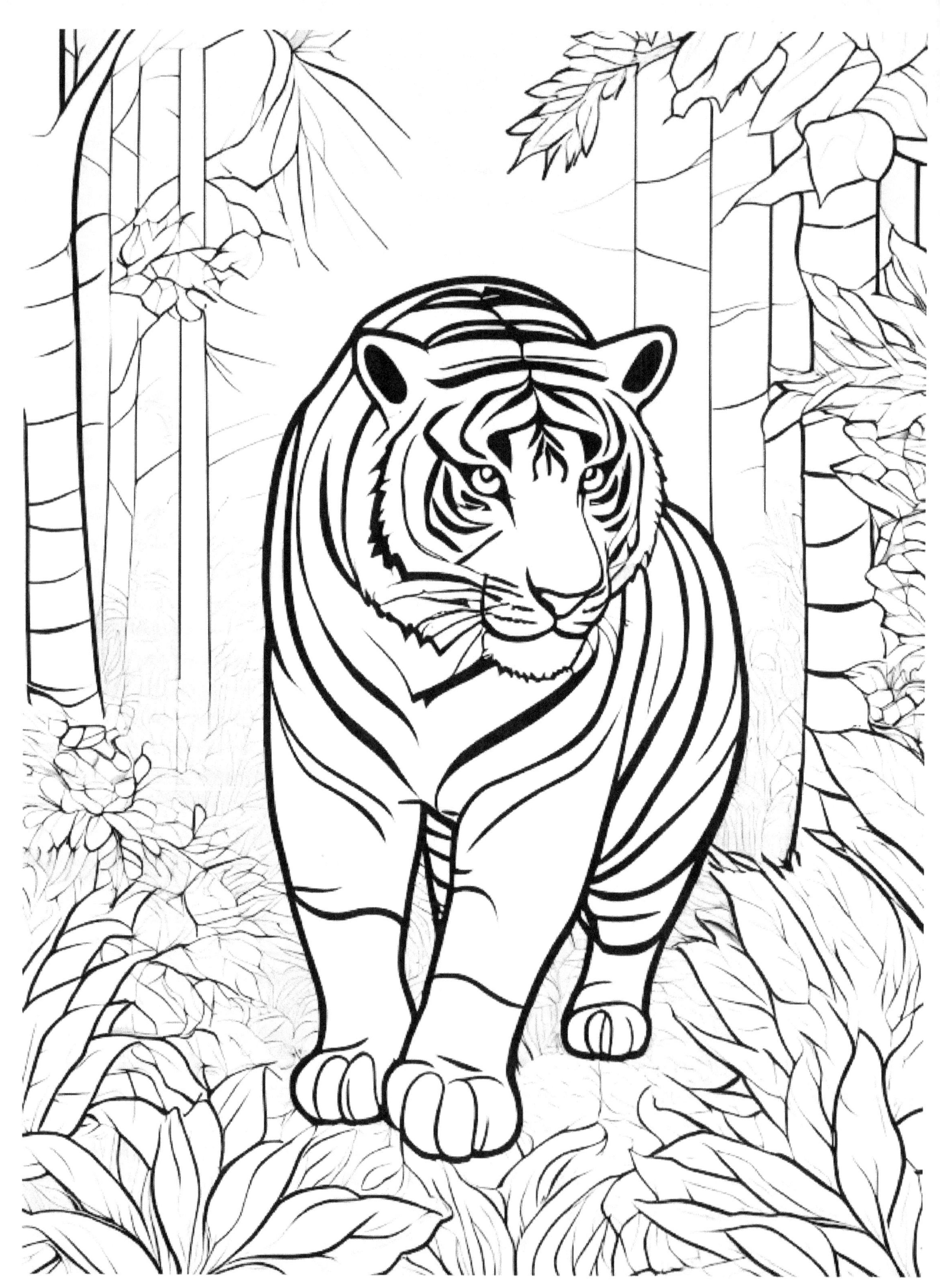

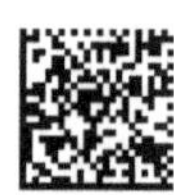